Dear Janet,

It is a pleasure working with you & getting to know you over the years! We are very lucky to have you ♡

Rumni

3/11/15

Blue Sky for All

A Book of Cooking & Compassion

Rumni Saha

authorHOUSE®

AuthorHouse™
1663 Liberty Drive
Bloomington, IN 47403
www.authorhouse.com
Phone: 1-800-839-8640

Published by AuthorHouse 12/02/2014

ISBN: 978-1-4969-5240-0 (sc)
ISBN: 978-1-4969-5239-4 (e)

This book is printed on acid-free paper.

About the Book

Blue Sky for All is a compilation of the wildly popular weekly column, "Kitchen Musings," by Rumni Saha, originally published in the Canton Citizen. In this book, Rumni shares her unique perspective on life, relationships, and current affairs while offering up a simple, delicious recipe for her readers.

This book is the author's hope for what its name expresses — a simple wish for a blue sky for all. The world that we live in is a fascinating place; it is up to us to seek and find the beauty and kindness of the people who live in it. We can all leave behind a lasting legacy of love and peace. By pushing aside the clouds that blind us, we can see the one and only one blue sky that we are all part of. Let's believe that kindness is not an option; let's be part of the Blue Revolution.

Liar, Liar September 20, 2012

I had taught my teenager to always be honest- why then did I feel elated when he made a dishonest move? While playing "Chutes & Ladders" with his 4-year old brother I watched him deliberately miscount so as to save his little "bro" from slipping down the slide when oh so close to the finish box. Just minutes later, bro got the much-needed number 3, which catapulted him to success. The simple words "Good Job Bro" & a pat on his proud back brought squeals of laughter & an unending announcement around the house. "I winned, I winned"- screamed the little guy; I smiled and discreetly congratulated my big guy savoring the sweet smell of *my* success.

For the next four weeks I will be sharing a few simple, no-fail dinner recipes with you. My hope is that these easy recipes will make your hurried life somewhat more manageable and slightly more flavorful. So here's to less time in the kitchen & more time at the kitchen table!

Slurping Good Hamburg Soup
(prescribed by Nurse Ducott)

1 Pound of Hamburg
1 quart of water
1 large can of chicken broth
1 cup of orzo
1 bag frozen mixed vegetables
1 large can diced tomatoes (28 ounces)
1 package of dry onion soup mix
1 tablespoon of Worcestershire sauce

Bring hamburg, water, and chicken broth to a boil for about 15 minutes. Add orzo, mixed vegetables, diced tomatoes, onion mix, and Worcestershire sauce and boil for an additional 20 minutes. Savor on a hurried fall evening.

Coexist September 27, 2012

Twin manatees balancing a mailbox, shocking pink flamingos frozen in time, lady bugs the size of coconuts, giant gnomes sprawled out in the sun, stoned birds in the birdbath next to the grinning bear, oversized plastic flowers with outstretched stems standing morbidly still in the window box, glassy fireflies, hummingbirds, butterflies and fairies- all under the watchful eye of a little lady in a leopard print jumper, lovingly tending her anarchic garden; perhaps in her mind's eye this is perfect harmony that we seek and not the chaotic imbalance that I see.

Simple Spaghetti (Fit for Lady Jules)

1-Pound spaghetti
6 slices of bacon
1 big onion chopped
½ cup of frozen peas
½ cup grated Parmesan cheese
Salt and pepper

Bring a large pot of water to a boil and add 2 tablespoons of salt. Drop the pasta into the boiling water and cook until al dente. Drain and set aside.

Meanwhile, in a large pan, fry 6 slices of bacon. Discard most of the fat and roughly chop the bacon when cool enough to handle. Set aside. Add the chopped onions to the pan and cook over medium heat, stirring frequently until it begins to caramelize.

Stir in the peas and cook, stirring, until it starts to brown. Add the bacon and stir to mix well. Add the pasta to the bacon/peas mixture and toss over medium heat until it is well coated. Remove from heat, stir in the cheese, and check the salt; adjust as needed and add fresh ground pepper.

Serve hot. (This dish freezes well. Freeze in individual serving containers so you can heat only what you need when you need it).

(Bacon tip- Cook a whole packet of bacon at one time; store 2-4 slices in individual freezer bags and pull out as needed).

Caterpetal (*noun*- a cross between a caterpillar and a flower inadvertently coined by a small family member) Oct 4, 2012

Every time my mutant teenager makes me mad beyond belief, it is in the image of a caterpillar that I find solace. Without a hairy, creepy, clumsy, caterpillar eating its way through life, there would be no beautiful butterfly spreading its delicate wings to take on the world looking for sweetness.

Good Goulash

2 small onions chunked
2 carrots chopped
1 stalk of celery chopped
1 sweet pepper & 1 Pound of mushrooms roughly chopped
2 cloves of garlic minced
2 lbs. of chicken chunked
3 tablespoons of tomato paste
1 can of (15 ounces) chickpeas rinsed & drained
2 cups of water
3 tablespoons of flour
2 tsp. paprika
1 tsp. Old Bay Seasoning
Salt & pepper to taste
Finely chopped Parsley

In about a tablespoon of oil, sauté roughly chopped sweet peppers and mushrooms; season with salt & pepper and set aside.

In a pan add 4 tbsp. of oil. Sauté chicken pieces (seasoned with paprika, salt and pepper and sprinkled with flour) until slightly browned. Set aside.

Add a tablespoon of oil and cook onions, carrots and celery till they begin to change color; add garlic and stir. Top with chicken pieces. In a small bowl combine tomato paste, and Old Bay seasoning and pour over chicken. Stir often till sauce mixture coats the chicken but make sure it does not burn. Add salt & pepper to taste. Add the chickpeas.

Add water; let it come to a boil. Cover and simmer on low heat for 15/20 minutes. Check for doneness. (Add peppers and mushrooms about 6 minutes before turning off the heat).

Add chopped parsley; served over egg noodles or rice.

You may use any kind of stew meat but remember to adjust your cooking time accordingly.

Tip: A tube of tomato paste (instead of a can) keeps well in the fridge ready for use anytime.

Happy To Hurt October 11, 2012

When asked how his day went, my little preschooler started sobbing inconsolably. "I was bad, I copied bad behavior in school today". Hysterical, he barely managed to get the words out. The **LOUDER** he cried, the **HAPPIER** I felt- the little man was growing up and so was his conscience!

Lazy Suzie's Quick and Easy Oriental Fish

1½-2 Pounds of fillet of white fish (e.g. Sole or Orange Roughy)
3 tablespoons of cornstarch
4 tsp. vegetable oil
4 tsp. soy sauce
2 tsp. vinegar
2 tsp. sugar
1 teaspoon Oyster sauce
1 cup of mushrooms roughly chopped
1 carrot- shredded
½ cup frozen peas
2 cups of thinly sliced scallions (diagonally chopped)
2 tsp. grated ginger root
2 tsp. minced garlic
(Canned vegetables such as bamboo shoots, baby corn- drained)

Cut fish into bite size pieces and marinate with 2 tsp. soy sauce; set aside for about 10 minutes. Add 3 tbsp. of cornstarch to the fish and mix well.

Heat the oil well. Lower the heat to moderate and add the marinated fish pieces and cook for about 3 minutes on each side or until they start to change into a golden brown color. Transfer to plate.

Add the veggies. Cook on high heat and cook until they start to become translucent. Add ginger and garlic pieces.

(You may also add chilly flakes for some heat). Add the peas and remaining canned vegetables. Cook for an additional 2 minutes.

Add 2 tsp. of soy sauce, 2 tsp. vinegar, 2 tsp. of sugar and 1 teaspoon of oyster sauce (remember to store the bottle in the refrigerator once opened). Add the fish and gently mix everything together.

Add the scallions and turn off heat.

Serve with steamed rice.

Tip: If you do not have Oyster sauce but must have this dish- go ahead & substitute Ketchup while you add Oyster Sauce to your shopping list. Also, you may use 1 cup of frozen oriental vegetables if you are really pressed for time.

Bird Brain- Think Again! October 18, 2012

Have you ever noticed that our friendly, neighborhood feathered friends are on an all-time Adrenaline high? I love birds not because they have the power to soar in the open skies but because they perpetually live on the edge and constantly flirt with danger. I have had many an encounter with many a bird as I am driving along, minding my own business when Little Tweety appears to jump out of nowhere headed straight for my windshield. As I look in horror to see the unthinkable, I see Tweety fluttering away instead, untouched, while I am left emotionally scarred and visibly shaken, even if only for a brief moment. And in my mind's eye, I can picture little Tweety Pie with an olive wreathe around its tiny bird brain racing up to its den to "tweet" about yet another super sucker!

It's apple season; every year I am awe-struck by the abundant display of these delicious and versatile culinary delights in our supermarkets and farm stands. There is something so nostalgic about these beauties that we want to bring them home even though we know that we will be canning them (or at least hoping to do so) for a long time to come! So for the next four weeks I will be sharing some of my favorite (and easy) apple recipes so you can put these pretty ladies to work. Do give these recipes a try; you will see that many of them will quickly become your own signature dish. By the way, I recently discovered Jazz Apples thanks to the nice produce guy at Stop & Shop. These sweeties certainly live up to their name!

Deliciously Easy Apple Crisp

3 Pounds of Cortland Apples
Cinnamon and Sugar Mixture
1 teaspoon of baking powder
1 cup of sugar
1 cup of flour

1 egg
1 stick of margarine or butter

Peel and slice apples.
Sprinkle with cinnamon & sugar mixture.
Place in a 13X9"pan (preferably glass).

Mix at high speed the sugar, flour, egg and baking powder until crumbly. Pour on top of apples. Then top with melted butter/ margarine. Bake for 45 minutes at 350° oven until lightly browned.

Thanks to Karen Harsfield for sharing this easy and always delicious recipe.

Tip: Make 2 batches at once and freeze one to pull out when you have that unexpected company.

All Rise October 25, 2012

It saddens me that ours is a world of copycats and unoriginals. You would think that diversity of characters and differences of personalities are what make life interesting. On the contrary, it now seems almost necessary for one to fit in instead of standing out, to belong instead of leading others. And God forbid if you are running for office! An important criterion for the position seeker then becomes his quality to fit in and act like every other person that he is trying to impress even if it means giving up the core values that he perhaps believes in deep down in his heart. Is it really worth acting like Dolly just to be revered by a million other Dollies?

I am sick of politicians acting like chameleons trying to blend in; I am sick of candidates walking on eggshells; I am tired of being told what I want to hear and not what you believe; I am sick of hypocrisy in every shape and form. Why do a crass stand-up routine or pretend to enjoy playing the ukulele or shamelessly bash those who dare to be different simply to make your fair-weather friends applaud for you-why not strive to do the right thing even if the person cheering for you is just one lone voice emanating from your heart?

Taffy Apples (A tasty treat to make & taste with your munchkins)

12/16 medium sized apples
1 cup of light corn syrup
2 cups of sugar
1½ cups of water
Red or seasonably orange food coloring
12/16 wooden Popsicle sticks

Wash and dry the apples and insert sticks. Place all ingredients together in a heavy saucepan over low heat. Stir until boiling. Let cool without stirring to 300° on a candy thermometer or to hardball stage.

Dip the apples in the syrup and place on waxed paper on a greased cookie sheet. Dip in coconut or sprinkles if desired.

Patricia Reilly's Amazing Apple Squares November 1, 2012

This week I want to share with you a simple recipe that calls for a can of Apple Pie filling. If you are someone who does not have time to shop every week but likes to keep a full pantry, go ahead and stock up on Apple Pie Filling. This recipe is also very versatile because it can be made with Cherry, Blueberry, or Pineapple Filling so you can make it to suit the taste of your family (or the state of your pantry).

This crowd-pleasing recipe was sent by Katie Healey, GMS Earth Science &Technology teacher. Katie has proudly shared with me what her mother Ms. Patricia Reilly, accomplished in a strange new world- a story that most of us can relate to. Along with unshakable values entrenched in our souls are lasting memories of family and good food and subsequently many cherished recipes that we are happy to pass along from generation to generation. The Apple Squares is one such recipe and the ordinary yet exceptional history of honest, hard-working people, who called it their own, makes it a wee bit sweeter.

Katie writes: "My mom came over alone by boat from Ireland at the age of 16 and lived with her Aunt and, now Canton resident, Isabella Browne who will be celebrating her 100th Birthday in January! She is an excellent cook who particularly enjoys baking for friends and family even to this day! She raised 8 children who are all adults now with their own families. Mom regularly bakes for family get-togethers and holidays and likes to make the favorites of her 20 grand children and one great granddaughter. This Apple Square recipe is one of her crowd-pleasing favorites and a favorite of many of the grand kids"!

Let's take a moment to raise our glasses to strong families and sweet treats!

With mixer cream together:
2 sticks of butter
2 cups of granulated sugar
1 teaspoon of vanilla

Add 4 eggs, one at a time beating well after each one. Fold in 3 cups of regular flour. Spread ½ - 2/3 of the dough on the bottom of a greased large cookie sheet. Spread 1 can of Apple Pie filling over batter. Dot the remaining batter on top of the filling and place in a 350° oven for one minute. Remove and spread batter over fruit. Bake for 35 minutes or until golden brown. Cut into 24 squares.

The Apple Squares are delicious warmed up in the microwave with a scoop of vanilla icecream.

Angels and Demon November 8, 2012

I greatly respected my next door neighbor for her unflinching faith which she brought to church every Sunday along with her perfectly mannered boys until I heard her at the pew one perfect Sunday morning quietly threatening her angels to "shut up and listen because God does not like rowdy, filthy children".

Here is a delicious spin on an old-fashioned Coffee Cake that will make you dizzy with excitement! Thank you to Jill A. for sharing Aunt Connie's treasure trove of recipes!

Aunt Connie's Apple Swirl Coffee Cake

5 apples, peeled and sliced
5 tablespoons of sugar
2 teaspoons of cinnamon
1 teaspoon of nutmeg
¼ cup of chopped nuts
3 cups of flour
2 cups of sugar
3 teaspoons of baking powder
1 teaspoon of salt
4 eggs
1 cup of vegetable oil
1 tablespoon of vanilla
¼ cup of Orange Juice

Combine apples, 5 tablespoons of sugar, cinnamon, nutmeg and nuts and set aside.

In a large bowl, place the flour, 2 cups of sugar, baking powder and salt.

In a separate bowl, beat the eggs, oil, vanilla, and Orange Juice until blended well. Add this to the flour mixture.

Pour ⅓ of the batter into a greased Bundt pan. Add ½ of the apples and then another ⅓ of the batter. Add remaining ½ of the apples and top with the last ⅓ of the batter.

Bake at 350° oven for about 1 hour 20 minutes.

Drizzle with icing (optional) while still warm and/or add crushed nuts. Recipe follows:

Combine ½ cup of Confectioners sugar, 1 teaspoon of melted butter, 1 teaspoon of vanilla and 2 tablespoons of milk. Combine till well blended.

Help yourself to a generous slice along with a steaming cup of coffee! Smile!

A Tumultuous Day November 15, 2012

Hurricane Sandy brought with it risky winds, restless rain and a surprise day off. In spite of a brief period of disappointment (because my initial reaction is to complain), I settled for "elated" with my unexpected gift from Mother Nature and Father Superintendent. I was going to use this free time to do –simply nothing!
Little did I know that "nothing" is a privilege that I can no longer afford. All day long I felt like mama bird incessantly flying in & out of her nest kitchen trying to quench the insatiable appetite of her hungry, squawking fledglings. For crying out loud, aren't these same creatures in school all day, perfectly satisfied with cold chicken nuggets and warm yogurt? What is it with the sight of Mama that makes these transformers hungry and mean?

And when the lights flickered suddenly and all went dark, I cried out in delight, trying hard to disguise my euphoria. At last I was being forced to do absolutely nothing. My empowerment at losing power was unfortunately short-lived; the lights came back on and with it a voice demanding "More Food"!

That night I was determined to rescue the sorry, trapped bird when all of a sudden I heard a sleepy chirp: "I love you Mama". It's then that I realized that life isn't so bad after all and every storm, even Sassy Sandy, has a silver lining.

The Lady Jules' Totally Terrific Turkey Burger

1 Pound turkey
1 egg
½ cup Italian style bread crumbs
½ cup cheddar cheese shredded
⅓ cup dried, sweetened cranberries

¼ cup of Parmesan cheese
1 tablespoon of garlic powder
salt and pepper

Combine all ingredients in a bowl...if on the wet side, add more bread crumbs: if dry and crumbly, add more egg. The consistency should be a medium paste--enough to form patties, sliders or meatballs. If cooking on grill, turn to medium high heat, if cooking on stove top, pre-heat metal pan and oil well. Allow oil to get hot. Cook through. Put on regular or slider buns (depending on your preference for size).

For Totally Terrific Topping:

1 goat cheese log
½ can cranberry jelly
½ cup mayonnaise (light works just fine)
½ cup toasted walnuts

Cut goat cheese in to ½ inch coins, and top each patty with 1-2 coins. Then combine next 3 ingredients thoroughly so that mixture is fairly homogenous. Top each patty with a healthy dollop of mayo.

Julie Stoltz is a Canton High School teacher, a close friend and an unbelievably creative cook. Julie's expert advise to you & me: "Edit as you would like, just give me credit :)!"

A Gentle Reminder November 22, 2012

Yes- I get it! Thanksgiving is a stressful time for many. Getting ready for a get-together, especially if you are the cook, the cleaner and in charge of throngs of thankless tasks can put a damper in the revelries. I am no preacher but one thing I know from experience - how a heart aches and pines for a family member who is too far away. So on Thanksgiving Day, even though Mom may still seem too overbearing, Aunt Judy just as judgmental, Dad a tad bit dated, and Uncle David undeniably unbearable, *let it go* and simply enjoy the togetherness. These are memories in the making, wild yet precious! Happy Holidays friends!

Easy Cheesy Turkey Chili (a packed with flavor chili, just in time for that painstakingly plentiful leftover turkey)

2 tablespoons cooking oil
1 onion, chopped
3 cloves garlic, minced
1 lb. boneless skinless leftover Turkey meat, cut into thin strips
2 tsp. chili powder
1 tbs. ground cumin
2 tsp. dried herbs like oregano
2 tsp. salt
1 jalapeno pepper, seeds and ribs removed, chopped (optional)
1 large can of crushed tomatoes with their juice
2 cups canned chicken broth
2- ⅔ cups drained black/red beans
½ tsp. fresh-ground black pepper
½ cup of shredded cheese

In a large saucepan, heat the oil. Add the onion and garlic; cook until they start to soften, about 4 minutes. Stir in the chili powder, cumin, oregano, salt and pepper. Add the turkey and cook to coat the spicy goodness. Add the jalapenos, the tomatoes with their juice and the broth. Bring to a boil, reduce the heat and stir in the beans. Simmer until the chili is thickened, about 15 minutes longer, covered.

Uncover the saucepan and stir in about ½ cup of cheese. Mix well & remove from heat. Top with cilantro & sour cream.

Other Suggested toppings

Who says corn bread, cranberry sauce, rolls, crushed chips, croutons, veggies and other leftovers from Turkey Day cannot accompany a steaming bowl of Chili? Go ahead and give it a try! Also, remember that this recipe is extremely forgiving; so feel free to play with it but don't forget to share if you stumble upon an amazing outcome!

Say Cheese November 29, 2012

I remember the day my little kindergartener came home from his first day at school a wee bit sad-the kind that only a mom can detect. Later that day I found out what was irking his little heart. "My teacher doesn't smile"- he said sadly as if this missing trait was the end of his kindergarten experience. Over the next few days Raunak grew to become fond of his teacher and enjoyed kindergarten immensely but even to this day he remembers Mrs. L. as "my teacher who never smiled". And though he is now older and somewhat wiser, the first thing he looks for to this day when he first meets someone is a smile. And even though I do not always agree with him and teach him never to judge a book by its cover, I cannot help but think that my little guy at age five had one thing right- a free smile is priceless and brightens up even the littlest heart.

Chocolate Chip Slices (makes 150 cookies)

6 eggs
½ cup shortening or margarine
1 Tbsp. vanilla
1 Lb. Confectioner's sugar
6 cups flour
1 Tbsp. baking soda
1 tsp. baking powder
1 tsp. cinnamon
12 oz. pkg. chocolate bits
1 to 2 cups walnuts- chopped

In a very large bowl beat together first 4 ingredients. Gradually add the dry ingredients. Stir in chocolate bits and nuts. The batter will be thick and sticky. For easier handling, refrigerate for an hour.

With floured hands shape into 6 loaves 1" high and 2" wide. Place 2 at a time on lightly greased sheets.

Bake at 375• for 12 to 15 minutes or until done. Do not overbake.

When cool glaze. When glazed (the loaves and you), cut into 1/2" slices.

Thanks to Aunt Connie for coming to the rescue again!

Life's a hoot December 6, 2012

I woke up at five this morning, took a shower, made my family breakfast, struggled with my son, barely packed him off to school, drove miles to my day job, stressed out at work, took a bite of my lunch, battled traffic again, came home to a pile of bills, homework, office work and a load of dirty dishes and best of all tomorrow and the day after will be the same. And you mean to say that I will not live for ever?

Cranberry Coffeecake (a traditional coffee cake with a festive twist**)**

½ cup Butter or Margarine
1 cup of sugar
2 eggs
2 cups of flour
1 teaspoon of baking powder
1 teaspoon of baking soda
½ teaspoon of salt
1 cup of sour cream
1 teaspoon of vanilla extract
1-16 ounce can of whole berry cranberry sauce

Preheat oven to 350°.

Grease and lightly flour (shaking off excess) tube or Bundt pan.

Beat in eggs, cream, butter and sugar.

Sift flour, baking powder, baking soda, and salt.

Mix sour cream and vanilla.

Alternately combine flour and sour cream mixture together.

Spread half of the batter in the pan.

Top with half of the cranberry sauce.

Add remaining batter and cranberry sauce.

Bake for 55 minutes.

Pat yourself on the back for this pretty creation!

Do unto others.... December 13, 2012

Growing up in a serene Eastern society, rebelling against all established values, I opposed all the age-old dictums that I was constantly bombarded with. I had heard the word "Karma" a million times but dismissed it casually every time as another shameless attempt on the part of some righteous pundit to bluff and blind us laymen. It was only after moving to America that frequent references to this overheard, overrated word by many a Westerner peaked my curiosity. What is this "Karma" that everyone refers to- I often pondered but wouldn't know until one day a simple payback made me believe that Karma is real and no twist of fate, and certainly no sham and no ordinary jargon. It was the time when I carelessly lost a few bucks that I was not willing to part with just minutes after telling the homeless man on the street that I had absolutely no change to spare. And once I connected my action and its reaction, I began to curiously run into many a misfortune for misconstruing the littlest, most harmless of facts. Well, call it making sense out of nonsense- I now believe that Karma doesn't just happen -it is I who makes Karma happen. Karma is nothing but my conscience beckoning me to be good and telling me that every action has an equal and opposite reaction, only this time it is the voice of Moral echoing the words of Newton.

Old World Raspberry Bars

2¼ cup of flour
1 cup of sugar
1 cup chopped pecans or walnuts
1 cup of butter or margarine
1 egg
A 10-ounce Jar of Raspberry Preserves

Preheat oven to 350°F. In a large mixing bowl combine all ingredients except raspberry. Beat at low speed until mixed well (about 2-3 minutes).

Reserve and set aside ½ cup mixture.

Press remaining mixture into greased 8" baking pan.

Spread preserves to within ½ "from edge of pan.

Spread reserved mixture on top of preserves.

Bake 40-50 minutes until lightly browned.

Cut into bars once cool.

My Mom December 20, 2012

What can I possibly begin to say something about someone who means everything to me? My "Ma" is truly the most amazing human being and after many rebellious teenage years when I tried to be nothing like her, I strive every minute today to be just like her. Ma was full of unstoppable energy until recently when that damned lump in her breast, sucked the lifeblood out of her. She was not supposed to make it out of that evil encounter but her dogged will would not accept defeat & she came back, slowly learning to do the things that she did so naturally, including cook. This is the woman who just three years ago was the living embodiment of the "Iron Chef", who could whip up the most delicious dish out of everything and nothing.

Growing up, the following chicken dish was a must at our celebration table during Xmas. Recently when I called Ma on the phone to let her know I had made it, she listened attentively & asked me to slow down so she could write down the steps. It brought tears to my eyes but in my heart I was grateful to have another regular conversation about food & family with my Ma…

Ma's Roasted Chicken with Signature Stuffing

1 Roaster Chicken
2 large potatoes- peeled & cubed (½" pieces)
1 small onion (finely chopped)
2 small tomatoes (chopped)
1 10 oz. package of mushrooms, roughly chopped

(Optional: A handful of chopped cashews and raisins; make sure to lightly fry them in a tablespoon of oil before adding them to the veggies).

In large pan, put 2-3 tablespoons of oil. Cook veggies until they begin to soften. Season with salt and set aside.

Pat salt & pepper over chicken & in cavity. Stuff the chicken with the signature stuffing once cooled.

Roast chicken according to package directions, basting with oil from time to time. (Add water to the bottom of the roasting pan and cook in a 350° oven with breast side up. e.g. 3 hours for a 6 Pound bird)

You may garnish the stuffing with sliced hard-boiled eggs before serving.

Enjoy the chicken, the stuffing but most of all - your family!

A Friend December 27, 2012

I have a friend who is smart, beautiful and talented but those are not the only reasons why I write about her. My friend stands out because even at her mature age she has managed to preserve a certain immaturity. Her eyes well up when we say goodbye even though she is right around the corner. She begs us to stay "just a little longer"' every time we are ready to leave even though there is always homework and housework to be done. She was the first one to nab my son when she found out that the little guy would be in dad's office all day in front of an iPad because the babysitter was sick. I yelled at dad for letting her have him on that particular day when she was particularly stressed over a million houseguests but he said she wouldn't have no for an answer. I thought she wasn't thinking - a classic her. She wants (and gets) lots of stuff but is the first one to part with the stuff if she senses that someone else wants it too. She is gorgeous yet genuinely believes that everyone around her is more beautiful than she is. Her piercing laugh is priceless and her tears are pure; there is no planning, no guile in what she does for others. I watch her zest for life and sometimes wonder who really is more mature, is it me with my meticulously calculated moves or is it her with her innocent, harmless recklessness? I think my immature friend has figured out life pretty well, more than mature me.

My Friend Lopa's Creamy Chicken Pasta

Penne Pasta: A pound
Grilled Cooked Chicken Breast pieces
Bell peppers (orange, red, yellow), cut into strips
2 cloves of garlic crushed
Salt and Pepper to taste
Asparagus Stems- 4 or 5
Bottle of Alfredo Sauce

Heavy Cream 1 cup
Lemon Juice: 1 teaspoon
Parmesan Cheese

Heat butter and olive oil in a pan. Add crushed garlic and crushed red pepper flakes to the pan. Add the chicken pieces and fry for some time. If you are using asparagus then this is the time to add them and fry with the chicken. Add the pepper slices and cook for some time but make sure the peppers don't lose color. Add half a bottle of Alfredo sauce and a cup of heavy cream. When you see bubbles around the edges, add salt, pepper and a teaspoon of lemon juice. Add the boiled penne to the cream mixture. Cook till the sauce thickens and coats the pasta. Take it off the fire and add a handful of grated Parmesan cheese. Serve hot with garlic bread.

PS: Use the Alfredo sauce and heavy cream to get to the desired consistency. You can substitute the chicken for shrimp.

Bon Appetito!!!

Pardon my French January 3, 2013

In this New Year may I politely remind you that the world would be a nicer place if people used more "F" words, Forgive and Forget, being two of my favorites?
Happy New Year Friends!

The following is one of the easiest and best fish recipes that I have tried. It comes from my son's best friend's mom. For the past ten years, I have seen this young, single mother of modest means struggle to raise her two young kids. Through all her ups & downs and her crazy busy schedule, she has managed to keep her focus on her kids. Another constant that she has tried to maintain is as many sit down dinners as possible- just the three of them. Over the course of the years, many snide remarks have been made by those who judge others by their worth in wealth. Today the kids are all grown, well on their way to becoming successful individuals. I know that the future generations will be a little brighter all because a young mother chose the right course- wicked stressful in the course of her life but fulfilling in the end. Kudos to the strong and loving women of this world! May we all strive to be more like them and less like those who judge them...

Baked Salmon with Cucumber Topping

1 pound of salmon fillet
1 cucumber
1 teaspoon of dried or fresh dill
2 tablespoons mayonnaise

Preheat oven to 350 degrees. Oil the bottom of a 9 x 13 baking pan. Cut cucumbers into tiny squares and mix with dill and mayonnaise. Rinse salmon with cold water and pat dry. Put salmon into baking dish and top with 1/2 of the cucumber salad. Bake in oven for about 20-25 minutes. Save cucumber salad to eat as a side with salmon. Serve with Risotto or Rice pilaf and a steamed vegetable.

The following article was written in honor of the angels of Newtown, CT.

Let's Wage Peace January 10, 2013

I heard the sickening news; I was mad and sad but mostly, in disbelief. All I wanted to do was to see my babies and forget that **that** ever happened. The yearning for this ordinary pleasure was irresistible; the guilt for this suddenly extraordinary craving was overwhelming.

Crippling pain is a state that even we, as adults, are never prepared to deal with. Imagine a child being flung into the midst of pure evil. Imagine hard working, do-good but utterly helpless professionals being caught in the throngs of unfathomable tragedy. There are no words to comfort them or those who have lost them.

Meanwhile the battle rages on as to how to prevent the unspeakable from happening again. All I know is that we cannot predict human intentions, especially those twisted beyond belief; we cannot cease evil but we certainly can seize the tool that evil has used over & over to carry out its senseless atrocities. There is nothing right about the right to bear arms if it has wronged millions. Assault weapons do not belong with lawless psychotics and pleasure-seeking lunatics; firearms belong in the safe arms of trained law enforcers. Let's remember this simple truth: guns are to kill just as lives are to live. Let's do everything in our power to make sure that innocent souls & selfless beings *did not* and *do not* die in vain. Let's wage peace.

Here's a recipe from the ultimate good guy – Canton's very own Police Chief, Ken Berkowitz. The Chief is the epitome of decency & integrity, a genuine everyday hero. We all know that he can cause a stir but who knew he could cook up a storm? Here's his signature Shepherd's Pie, a simple must-try dish that will make you a fan too! Thanks Chief and to the many unsung heroes who are quietly working to keep us safe!

Chief Berkowitz's Winning Shepherd's Pie

1 onion chopped
1½- 2 Pounds of Hamburger meat
1 Box (2 packets) of Instant Garlic Mashed Potatoes
1 Big package of Frozen Corn

Cook the potatoes according to package directions.

In a large pan, sauté the Hamburger meat with the onions.

Meanwhile, line the bottom of a baking dish with corn. Put the cooked hamburger meat over the corn and spread the potatoes on top.

Bake the casserole for about 30-45 minutes in a 350° oven. Put the casserole under the broiler for the last 5 minutes for an extra crispy topping.

Let cool & cut into squares. Enjoy!

Father, Philosopher & Guide January 17, 2013

There is nothing more precious than watching a four year old unable to contain his excitement when Daddy praises his very modern art. Daddy's simple lies of "No way you did this by yourself" are enough to launch the little shrimp onto the ceiling. At "I am ***so*** proud of you" the little creature flaps his wings, a mile a minute, reminiscent of a little bird getting ready to fly. Quietly watching this (un)pretentious interaction between man & son, I realize that this abstract piece of preschool art is a concrete foundation to character-building taking shape before my very eyes.

Packed with flavor Chicken Roll(ups)

Tortillas, one for each diner
2 cups deboned Rotisserie chicken chunks
A quarter onion, chopped
2 cloves of fresh, minced garlic

1 tbsp. of Tandoori Powder- available in the International section of your grocery store. If you cannot find Tandoori Powder, you may add 1 tsp. each of Cumin and Coriander powder.

Chilly powder-a pinch

Pain yoghurt/mayonnaise, ketchup, (1 tablespoon each for each tortilla), chopped lettuce, tomatoes, onions, green/red peppers, jalapenos, chopped cilantro or any other veggies to your liking.

In a heated pan:

Add 1 tablespoon of oil.

Add onions. Fry till they start to change color.

Add garlic, cumin, coriander (or Tandoori Powder) and chili powder. Cook for about 2 minutes making sure the garlic doesn't brown. Add the chicken pieces & cook for about 5 minutes, stirring well to coat. Transfer to another plate.

Wipe down the pan with paper towel.

Add a drop of oil in pan (for each tortilla). Heat & spread around. Add tortilla and let each side cook for about a minute or till it starts to get a nice golden color.

On a plate, lay down the toasted tortilla.

Spread a tablespoon of plain yoghurt or mayonnaise, ketchup or hot sauce and the chicken stuffing. Pile on the fresh veggies. Roll up and enjoy the extraordinary flavors of an ordinary store-bought chicken.

Wild Thing January 24, 2013

Who knew that an unruly, unwelcome houseguest would teach me a thing or two about tenacity? It all started when Rocky decided to make nightly stops inside my garbage can expecting dinner & clean up afterwards. This would have been quite cute if he weren't so messy. My poor man, although sympathizing with Rocky, came home armed with ample ammunitions to maintain domestic peace: a raccoon proof trashcan and raccoon repulsing bags. The price tag alone was going to take care of that belligerent bugger!

That night the riot outside informed me that my nightly regular was back. As the lights flickered outside from the motion detector I caught a glimpse of the masked bandit in a raving rage. As I sneered at him from the comfort of my home he growled ferociously back at me before disappearing into the darkness.

The next morning, I noticed happily that although the trash was nervously resting on its side the lid was still intact. At last, I had won the battle that had been raging for much too long! However as I came closer I was dismayed to see my driveway speckled with leftovers. As I approached the trash to survey the cause of the damage, I noticed that Rocky, in his determination to get to me & my tossed out goodies, had chewed through the lid and even though he couldn't twist it, his angry choppers had made a large enough door that allowed him entry into his diner for a cozy moonlight dinner. Proof of his midnight madness was strewn all around, the scribbling of his dirty paws did not seem apologetic in the least but even though I was mad at first, I couldn't help but laugh at the dogged determination of a wild thing to reach his destination by hook or by crook. And only last night I heard that all too familiar tap-tapping unmistakably coming from my head; Rocky has now moved closer to his favorite diner- to the roof-top penthouse.

My Friend Sabina's Apple Cake

4 cups of chopped apples, 2 cups of sugar

Let apples and sugar sit for 3 hours at least. Overnight is fine and works well. Next day preheat oven to 350°. Mix apples and sugar with

2 cups of flour, 2 eggs, 2 teaspoons of baking soda, 1 teaspoon of cinnamon, 1 cup of oil and 1 cup raisins or nuts.

Pour into a greased and floured 13 x 9 baking pan. Bake until done (about 30 minutes) until knife comes out clean. Yummy!

Life is a Highway... January 31, 2013

This morning as I was driving to work I came across a horrible sight. The all too familiar highway had become the site of a three-car accident with two of the cars piled atop each other like discarded laundry. I shuddered at the sight of what appeared to be the mangled remains of a red car and a driver in red. I froze as my ears picked up the siren of a speeding ambulance and my rear-view mirror the lights of a racing police car. I couldn't help but think about the many lives that would be damaged hereafter along with those destroyed in that crash. I also remember thinking that my life would permanently slow down from that moment on just like the traffic around me, which had come to a halt - a staggering combination of curiosity, deference and disbelief.

This afternoon I passed by the same fateful spot as I made my way back home. The traffic had resumed to its normal speed, the space had been cleared of the frightful debris, and there was no vestige of that early morning mess. Life is so merciless and yet so forgetful and yes- although life may stop momentarily, it does go on forever- just like the tireless traffic on I-95.

Thai Thighs

1 pound of skinless, boneless chicken thighs cut into 1" pieces (breasts work fine but Thai Thighs sound better!) Sprinkle with salt and about 2 tablespoons of cornstarch
1 big onion roughly chopped
6 cloves of garlic minced
1 large red pepper cut into 2" pieces
½ can of coconut milk (unsweetened, available in the International section of your supermarket)
½ cup of chicken broth

4-5 springs of scallions
Soy Sauce (2 tablespoons)
Oyster Sauce (2 tablespoons)
Vegetable oil

In about 1 tablespoon of oil, add onions and cook till they start to change color slightly. Add garlic pieces, stirring so they don't burn and then add pepper pieces. Cook for about 2 more minutes and then set aside in a separate container.

Add 2 tablespoons of oil, add the chicken pieces till they change color slightly. Add Soy Sauce, Oyster Sauce and cook till chicken is well coated. Add coconut milk and broth; lower heat and let simmer for about 20 minutes on low setting. Add scallions and cooked onion/pepper mixture and simmer for another 5 minutes. Mix well and serve with white rice.

Extreme Sports February 7, 2013

Tell me there is nothing wrong with the following:

1. One of the most admired athletes of all times delivering a calculated confession to years of doping & lying.
2. No one inducted into the 2012 Baseball Hall of Fame due to rumored drug use.
3. Four NFL players taking their own life (and some, the life of others before that).
4. An NHL lockout for months with complete disregard to those who matter- the fans.

   These are the folks who get paid in millions. These are the heroes who we all look up to. These are the idols that kids dream of becoming some day.

   Am I missing something or is sportsmanship missing from sports?

Extreme Gourmet Sandwiches

Hearty Bread like Torta Roll
1 small Jar of Pesto
1 Jar of Roasted Red Peppers (3/4 pieces for each sandwich)
2 Pounds of Chicken Breasts marinated in the following:
1 Package of Onion Soup Mix
Minced garlic (4 cloves)
Italian Spice Blend
Pinch of chilly powder
½ cup Red Wine Vinegar
Salt & Pepper to taste

Chicken may be marinated overnight or for a couple of hours. Grill and cut into strips.

On each side of the toasted bread put a Tbs. of Pesto, pile grilled chicken pieces and top with Roasted Red peppers. Healthy, filling and bursting with flavors!

A Love Letter February 14, 2013

The honeymoon ended briefly after the marriage and reality set in, sometimes harsh but mostly real. Many moons and many compromises later, blind love has been replaced by affection, fire by fondness, romance by respect, and puppy love by dogged emotions.

The teenager for whom I forsook two young parents, takes care of the not-so-young parents today, the youngster who stole my heart & needed me at all times has time for his own young ones today, the unmatched athletic powers have been replaced by rock solid mental prowess.

Life goes on and even though it is not always exactly how I pictured it would be in my 13 year-old eyes, I am grateful to have & to hold my "old" knight in shining armor. The road is not always smooth but there is a certain peace knowing that he holds the unseen net below me in case I tumble.

The heart is a powerful thing; listen to it when it speaks to you. I am glad I did.

Happy Valentines Day to all of us!

Here's a quick dinner that is sure to win any heart. Enjoy!

Rustic Chicken Hash

2 boneless chicken breasts
1 large red onion (chopped)
2 large potatoes (diced into 1" pieces)
4 cloves garlic
2 red/green bell peppers (roughly chopped)
1 cup of scallions (roughly chopped)
1-cup cherry tomatoes (halved)

2 Tbs. tomato paste
Fresh parsley

Poach chicken in water seasoned with salt & pepper till tender but not falling apart. Roughly chop once cooled.

In a large pan, put a quarter stick of butter & 1 Tbs. olive oil. On medium heat, sauté the onion, potatoes and then add garlic. When potatoes are almost tender add the bell peppers. Season with salt & pepper; add 1 Tsp. paprika and tomato paste. Add sautéed chicken & stir-fry till spices coat the pieces & start to change color. Add cherry tomatoes and cook for another 5 minutes with cover on. Turn off heat & add scallions & parsley. Enjoy over a plate of steaming rice or with a slice of thick, hearty bread.

Fighting fear Feb 21, 2013

There is no doubt that however educated we claim to be, in some ways, we are all ignorant. Often we are afraid of things we do not understand or do not take the time to understand. The solution is simple-take the time to know and learn and you will find that there is no need to be afraid. I used to be terrified of people with mental disabilities (shameful), I used to be afraid of gays and lesbians thinking that they might rub off on me (sinful), I used to be scared of people with darker skin than me and people with lighter skin than mine, I used to be nervous around a million other people for a million other reasons till I took a moment to know them and then I found that I should have been afraid of no one but me all along. There is no bigger danger than ignorance itself.

Meat Pie

1 Pound of Ground Beef
1 stalk of celery including leaves- cut into small pieces
2 carrots (shredded)
1 large onion- sliced
1 Package (2 shells) of 9" Pie Shell (store brand works fine)
1 egg beaten (you only need a little bit)

In a Tbs. of oil, sauté, onions and ground beef. Add a stalk of rosemary leaves (no stems please). Add remaining veggies and cook until tender & the meat is no longer pink. Add 1 Tbs. of mustard, 1 Tbs. of Worcestershire Sauce, salt & pepper and 2 Tbs. of flour. Stir well and add a 14 oz. can of Beef Broth. Let simmer for 15 minutes or until most of the broth is absorbed. Add 2 Tbs. of butter to give it a rich flavor.

Let cool.

In a 9" pie pan, lay a 9" pre-made pie shell. Prick the bottom of the shell 2/3 times and bake at 450° for 15 minutes.

Reduce the oven temperature to 350°. Add the Pie mixture on the bottom of the pie shell, top with remaining 9" shell. Try to crimp & tuck the edges under the cooked shell.

Brush the top with the beaten egg.

Bake for about 30/40 minutes or until the top turns golden brown. Take care not to overcook it. Let cool. Cut into wedges (6-8) and serve with mashed potatoes, peas or a simple salad.

Wake Up February 28, 2013

I was at a wake this afternoon. It was a surreal sight; family members standing in attention while scores of loved ones snaked around to catch one last glimpse of the young man. It was a heart-wrenching experience; yet I got into my car afterwards and laughed my heart out. I was thrilled that I had been given more time- don't know how much but enough to bury the truth about death.

No Fail Coffee Cake

1½ Tsp. baking powder
½ Tsp. baking soda
1-cup (½ Pound) butter or margarine at room temperature
1¼ cups sugar
2 eggs
2 cups all-purpose flour
1-cup low fat plain yogurt or sour cream
1 Tsp. vanilla
¾ cup finely chopped walnuts
1 Tsp. ground cinnamon

In a medium bowl, mix flour, baking powder, baking soda and set aside.

In a large bowl, beat butter, 1¼ cups sugar and eggs with an electric mixer until creamy. Stir in flour mixture and add vanilla, yogurt/sour cream until well blended. Spoon half the batter evenly into a greased and floured 9" tube or Bundt pan.

In a small bowl, mix together the walnuts, 1 Tbs. sugar and cinnamon. Sprinkle half of the nut mixture over the batter; Spoon in the remaining batter and top with nut mixture.

Place in a COLD 350° oven and bake for about an hour until a wooden pick inserted in the center of the cake comes out clean. Enjoy- life is too short!

Hello friends,

The other day a casual conversation with a colleague left me feeling somewhat guilty. Turns out that I have been, unintentionally of course, ignoring the vegetarians of Canton. To make up for my shortcomings, I plan to dedicate the next four weeks to determined folks like Donna who have chosen a healthier life-style. I also dedicate the following article to the strong-willed amongst us. Your resolve is commendable!

Love,
Rumni

Fateful Blizzard March 7, 2013

I needed the Blizzard of 2013 to renew my faith in--me. After years of living with myself, I had started to take me for granted, the good with the not so good. There were many simple things like exercising that I had started to avoid--claiming that there was simply no time or that my elbow, which lately has become quite the bone of contention in an otherwise healthy body, could not handle it.

As I looked out of my window at the wintry heap that the Blizzard had dumped, I was convinced that I would have to stay indoors until spring. There was no way I could shovel my way out of this mess. I cursed the plough driver for dumping more snow at the mouth of my driveway than Mother Nature herself. I plotted to take down the gloating town worker; I dreamed of moving to balmier climates but first--I would have to get out.

I went outside armed with a shovel and a determination that I thought no longer existed. The first "whack" of the shovel was the most painful, my elbow almost gave way, but gradually the pain started numbing as the ground started revealing itself. It was no mean feat, interjected by many expletives, but after many hours of non-stop, backbreaking work, it was complete. What had seemed like an impossible task when I first peered out of my window had now become possible!

Soon thereafter, I collapsed on my couch, an aching mess but secretly rejoicing at the lesson learned. I was broken but at the same time stronger than ever before and I was convinced that this renewed faith would help me do anything I set my mind to.

It has been four weeks since my enlightenment--now if only someone could convince me that my knee would not give in if I ran on that treadmill…

Pasta Perfect

2 large zucchinis- cut into 1½" pieces
1 medium sized eggplant- cut into small, diagonal pieces
1 small onion- sliced
A handful of cherry tomatoes
2 garlic cloves- finely chopped

Season the zucchini & eggplant pieces with salt & pepper, add a Tsp. of olive oil and grill-- till marks appear. You may sauté them if you do not have a grill/grill pan.

Cook a package of whole grain spaghetti according to directions and drain, reserving about a quarter cup of the pasta water.

In a large pan heat about 2 Tbsp. of olive oil; add the garlic pieces, onions, a few pepper flakes and then the tomatoes. Add the grilled veggies. Season with salt & pepper. Add fresh or dried seasonings of your choice (e.g. Parsley, Thyme or your favorite blend).

Add the cooked pasta to the veggies, the pasta water and check for salt & pepper. Serve hot with shavings of freshly grated Parmesan cheese.

Once Upon This time March 14, 2013

My two boys, aged 4 & 14, can get along fine for just under 4 minutes. Believe me--I have enough data to corroborate this thesis. What starts out as a bear hug invariably ends in a grizzly attack, one more vicious than the next. Before you start looking up "Family & Social Services", please know that it is just as hard for me not to do the same for the next 4 minutes, at which point they turn into the gentlest & cuddliest baby bears again.

Quickie Quesadillas (QQs)

Ingredients:
1-cup salsa
Fresh veggies like red onions, zucchini, green/red peppers, tomatoes, cilantro, frozen corn and sliced jalapenos for a kick
2 cloves of garlic
4 flour or wheat tortillas
½ cup shredded Monterey Jack cheese or any shredded cheese

In a Tbsp. of oil, add the chopped onions, garlic, peppers, zucchini and corn. Sauté till they begin to change color. Let cool. Assemble tortillas by putting a layer of veggies, extra jalapenos, salsa, cheese & cilantro. Grill or cook folded tortilla on a lightly oiled skillet till it turns a golden brown color. Serve with sour cream & salsa. (Another shortcut is to stuff one tortilla with all the desired ingredients and cover with a second tortilla, taking care to put cheese around the edges which will act as a glue). Fell free to substitute any of the above veggies with your favorites.

Shhhhh... March 21, 2013

Here I am clamoring for equality with the opposite sex yet I choose to be different from my male counterpart in a certain way.

A lone trip back from a shopping spree often ends in a surreptitious entrance into the house with a quick stopover in the coat closet. I move with the stealth of an undercover agent with the intent of hiding half of my newfound treasures particularly those I intend to adorn myself with. Sometimes the hands-free entrance is extra bold declaring a "no-win, no-find, boring experience" because the bag of goodies has been casually camouflaged in the trunk of the trusted car. It baffles me as to why I am tempted to plot & hide even though I know that my man does not give a damn. If anything, he is rather dismayed at the idea of me roaming the malls for hours on end only to return with absolutely nothing. My poor guy on the other hand comes back from his rare shopping trip armed with a bag of practical must-haves, which he promptly hands over to me with the innocent question "What do you think?" What I think is that he is shamelessly honest & that I am shamefully ashamed but I am painfully aware even at that guilty moment that this exchange will have no lasting impact on me. I solemnly swear to be faithful and share all my love (and yes- all the heartaches) but some things are best not shared...

Baked Frittata

Ingredients:
16 eggs (You may also use Only Whites)
1 green pepper
1 red pepper
1 cup of mushrooms

1½ cups of cut up asparagus or diced zucchini or your choice of veggies
1 large onion
½ cup breadcrumbs
2 cups grated cheese
Parsley (fresh or dried)
Salt and pepper
2 tbsp. olive oil

Sauté onions in olive oil. Add peppers and zucchini and cook for about 4 minutes. Add mushrooms and cook for an additional 2/3 minutes. Add salt, pepper and parsley for seasoning. Shut off stove and set aside vegetables for cooling.

Beat eggs with salt and pepper, adding cheese and breadcrumbs (but save 1/4 cup of breadcrumbs for later).

Grease 9x11" pan with oil or spray.

Sprinkle the remaining breadcrumbs onto the bottom of the pan.

Add eggs and vegetables to pan.

Bake at 350-375° for 20-30 minutes. When a knife comes out clean from the center of the frittata, you know it's done.

Remove from oven and let it sit for 15 minutes before cutting. Enjoy!

High Society March 28, 2013

Recently I was at a party- a festive celebration that quickly turned bizarre. Instead of mingling while waiting for others to arrive, the folks gathered decided to do what modern, smart people do- navigate new territories via their smart phones. I was naïve thinking that this virtual tour would come to an end once the party started for that's when more partygoers began checking their social networking sites. Apparently, a cyber stop at a cyber spot with simulated interaction was more stimulating than old-fashioned chat. One guest, in particular, had a veritable glazed look, which seemed to be cured temporarily each time she partied with her cyber friends. Yet another felt compelled to share with me quite the empty words of wisdom someone else had posted. At one point the hostess herself was in the kitchen busy texting although she delightfully claimed that all her friends were gathered together in her living room.

This was supposed to be a night of mindless fun yet my mind was inundated with lofty questions: Why did so many feel the urge to "chat" with faceless people when the room was teeming with familiar faces? Why was everyone so lonely in a room full of friends? Why wasn't everybody bothered by what, only recently, would have been unacceptable behavior? And the most troubling of them all-was everyone around me socially inept or had ***I*** somehow turned into the awkward one? That evening's happenings got me thinking but I am happy to report, after days of pondering, that **smart** phones & fancy gadgets do not make me **wiser** and what I really want to do is "party like it's 1999"!

Here are two simple side dishes from a young lady who is destined to be a wonderful and caring teacher someday. Thank you Miss Alicia for your passion for everything you do!

Pretty Salad

Can of black beans- drained & rinsed
Grape tomatoes (about 8-10)- cut into quarters
Red onion- 1 small (chopped)
Juice of 2 Limes
Plain frozen corn- 1 bag (cooked according to directions)
Cilantro

Mix everything and add salt & pepper to taste. Great accompaniment to a veggie burger!

Awesome Casserole

2-16 oz bags of frozen broccoli
2 Cream of Mushroom soup cans
1 Box of French Fried onions
1 bag of Swiss Cheese

Mix everything (Save some crunchies for topping) together and put in a 350° oven. Bake for 30 minutes with foil on. Bake an additional 30 minutes with foil off & crunchies on.

Yummy!

We the Papal April 4, 2013

The west never misses an opportunity to voice its opinion about how poorly the east treats its women. But why then, in this progressive western world, is the female voice silenced when it comes to choosing the leader of an organization, two thirds of whose members are females (which amounts to a whopping eight hundred million of us)? Why, when a woman can be trusted to serve in every field imaginable, is she shunned from choosing the leader or better still, being the leader in a field which preaches love, compassion & fairness to all? But wait- am I that naïve to imagine even for a moment, a woman heading an organization of 1.2 billion members when she can't even be trusted to lead my neighborhood place of worship? Unfortunately, there is nothing holy about double standards. I have no problem with the Big Guy- only with the little guys who serve Him (& Her).

Wake up your Taste Buds Breakfast Popovers

2 tablespoons oil
1-Pound Italian sausage
2 cloves garlic, minced
2 cups shredded Mozzarella- divided
4 large eggs
2 cups milk
1-½ cups of all-purpose flour
2 small green onions
3 Tbsp. chopped fresh parsley
2 cloves of garlic-minced
1-Tsp salt
1-Tsp pepper
Large or medium sized muffin pans

Preheat to 400•. Grease the muffin cups well.

Heat the oil. Add the sausage and break up with spoon. Cook until brown and cooked through. Spoon about 2 tablespoons sausage into each muffin cup. Sprinkle about 1½ Tbsp. of cheese on top of the sausage.

Blend the eggs in a blender until frothy, about 20 seconds. Add the milk, flour,1 cup of cheese, garlic, green onions, parsley, salt and pepper. Blend until mixed together. Pour the batter into the muffin cups, filling each cup to just below the top. Bake, without opening the oven door, until puffed and golden, about 30 minutes.

Serve hot; just as delicious reheated the next morning.

Pioneer Woman April 11, 2013

My dear friend Jill is a wild woman with a tame heart large enough to house all the lonely animals of the world. She has an almost childlike obsession with horses and "all things cowgirl". She also has a grownup passion for children and teaching. She is a perky personality, a vibrant spirit and owns a deliciously twisted sense of humor. Those who know her would easily agree that "generosity" could well be her middle name. What more can you ask for in a person? Oh yeah- she is an awesome cook and the following recipe comes from her.

I am writing about Jill not because she has shared with me many fabulous recipes (not to mention her blessed Aunt Connie's Treasure Trove of Family Favorites), but to say that sometimes friendship can forge in the most unlikeliest of places. You see- Jill was my boss once upon a time and we did not always see eye to eye; in fact there was a time when I was ready to quit my day job because of our very difficult relationship. I am glad that we were able to get past our differences and forge a friendship that, I am proud to say, is here to stay. I think it was because Jill kept her big heart open and never closed her mind; so for those of you who are struggling with relationships (personal or professional)- know that all is not hopeless even though it appears so. You have a lot to gain simply by unleashing the cowgirl (or cowboy) in you and keeping your mind's window open. You will see new territories opening around you and green pastures that will soothe your weary heart.

Thank you to kind souls like Jill who make this world more livable for humans and animals alike!

Jill's Chicken Soup for the Soul

2 whole chicken breasts (bone in)
3 hearts of celery and 2 packets of carrots- chopped into bite-size pieces
2 packages of Onion Soup Mix
2 packages of Lipton Double Noodle Soup
1 cup of Ditalini Pasta
Put chicken in pot filled with water. Add salt.

Let boil for ½ hour to 45 minutes. Carefully take chicken out, take skin & bones off and cut into bite sizes. Add veggies and cook until tender. Add the packages of soup mix. Let cook; add chicken pieces back in and cook till everything comes together. Season with salt & pepper. Add broth if too thick. In a separate pot cook the pasta; add to soup just before serving. Enjoy!

Radio gaga April 18, 2013

Is anyone out there bothered by the lewd and lurid lyrics on the radio these days? I certainly didn't find it cute when I heard a 4- year old mouth off some very inappropriate & unsuitable words to a chart-topper with a certain swagger that guaranteed a star on the Hollywood Walk of Fame some day. Of course he had no idea what the seemingly innocent words meant; before long a gaggle of preschoolers joined in the chorus. I turned to the adult next to me with obvious dismay but she admonished me for being "too uptight". "Everyone listens to this kinda music today", she added. "She's right, I am being neurotic", I consoled myself as I overheard little Mikey, standing near the sandbox, shout "Let's get dirty" but quickly updated my status to "justifiably uptight" as the words "And sweat until my clothes come off" caught my ears.

Kid-Friendly Applesauce Breakfast Cake

¼-cup packed brown sugar
1 Tbs. butter or margarine at room temperature
½- Tsp. ground cinnamon
¼-cup chopped walnuts or raisins
1 cup of flour
⅓-cup sugar
½-Tsp. Baking Powder
¼-tsp. Baking Soda
1 egg
½-cup Applesauce
¼-cup cooking oil
½-Tspn. of Vanilla

Preheat oven to 350°. Grease a 9x11" baking pan.

Mix together dry ingredients and set aside.

Beat egg until smooth. Add Applesauce, oil and Vanilla to combine well.

Stir Applesauce mixture to dry ingredients; mix well. Pour the batter to the pan.

Make the topping of brown sugar, butter/margarine, and cinnamon. Use hands to mix together till mixture is crumbly and then add nuts/raisins.

Sprinkle topping to batter.

Bake for 20-25 minutes until toothpick inserted comes out clean.

Enjoy munching with your munchkins!

E is for…. April 24, 2013

Today I wish to be neither clever nor funny; my sole mission in honor of Earth Day is to inform kind souls like you about a systematic genocide of the smartest species on earth taking place as we speak.

I dedicate this column to the most emotional of all living beings- the elephants, with the hope that you will be inspired to take up their cause. Did you know that the number of elephants, whose population was well over 10 million during the 1930s in the African Plains alone, has dwindled to about half a million? Today these magnificent animals are turning up on the plains of Africa—headless. These beautiful creatures---the age-old symbols of power & wisdom, are powerless and tethering on the brink of extinction-- all because some heartless, rich goon with a twisted taste wants his ivory trophy.

Elephants are able to think critically, problem-solve, communicate, display emotions just like us and possess memories far superior than ours. The heart-wrenching part in all of this is that these animals understand perfectly that they are being slaughtered; they are aware of their impending destiny and they are mourning their plight. Scientists say that the once playful, carefree species is now displaying signs of PTSD and acting the same way as people living in a warzone.

The annihilation of an innocent species in the hands of humans in the 21st century is reprehensible. If we do not do something to stop this senseless killing we will soon be teaching our children, fascinated with these gentle giants that "E is for Extinction" instead of "for Elephants".

For more information on this topic please read National Geographic's "Blood Ivory". It is time for our species to help another that desperately needs our help. And seriously, if we had the insight (& the brains) to send a man to the moon, we certainly should have the foresight (& the smarts) to save these majestic creatures from disappearing from this earth.

Happy Earth Day Everyday friends!

Refreshing Mango Smoothies

2 cups plain yogurt
1 cup of cold milk
¼ cup sugar (or 2 Tbsp. Honey)
1 cup of mango puree or 1 large ripe mango or 4 mango slices from a jar

Blend everything together in a blender. Enjoy the most refreshing drink just in time for spring.

Peace- an alien concept? May 3, 2013

The same time our hearts were aching for innocence violated, NASA reported a significant discovery- three new Earth-like planets "whose size and location are right for sustaining life".

For a moment the horror of the Boston massacre left me and I was filled with hope. What if these planets hold a life form that is superior to ours, where there are no man-made boundaries, no disparity, where peace is the norm and compassion the rule of law? What if the residents of these planets do not have the concept of cruelty and where no one experiences sickness or pain, where everybody lives together- happily ever after? What if there really is such a place that Lennon wanted us to "Imagine"?

It is heart-breaking that mankind has morphed into something that is anything but kind. Our superior intelligence is being channelized to strike terror and inflict pain towards our brothers and sisters. What has our world come to? We need divine intervention, perhaps in the form of aliens who can teach us to be human again.

Mexican Rice

2 tomatoes (quartered)
½ green pepper (roughly chopped)
1 medium onion, peeled and quartered
3 garlic cloves
1 jalapeno (seeded)
1 quarter bunch of cilantro leaves
1 packet of Sazon seasoning (optional) or 1 Tbsp. of cumin
2 cups white rice
1 can of red or black beans (drained & rinsed)
4 Tbsp. of oil

4 cups chicken broth (water works too)
Salt to taste
1 lime, cut into wedges

In blender, blend the first 6 ingredients with a dash of water.

Heat the oil and add the spice blend. Fry well stirring frequently. Add cumin/sazon.

Add rice and sauté, stirring frequently, until rice is golden brown.

Add the can of drained beans and the broth/water.

Cover the pot and let simmer until rice is fully cooked (about 20 minutes).

Serve with lime wedges.

(You may make this a one pot-meal by adding pieces of chicken to the spice mixture & sautéing before adding the rice).

Happy Cinco de Mayo friends- let's live life to the fullest!

Words to Live by May 10, 2013

Today my little guy asked me how many kinds of humans there are. Taken aback, I answered "Just one", but curious to find out the thinking behind this random questioning, I prodded him as to what he meant. He answered, matter-of-factly, "I knew it was only one but I wish humans were like animals —some striped, some spotted, and all different colors. Doesn't that make the animal kingdom ***so*** cool, mom?" As I looked into my baby's big, brown eyes gleaming with pure wonderment, I prayed that this zest for "all things different" stay with him well past these wonder years.

Happy Mother's Day to us all!

My Mama's Coconut Shrimp Curry

Marinate 1 Lb. of shrimp (Tail-on or off) in the following for an hour or overnight: Paste of ½" ginger root, ½ small onion, 1- Tsp. cumin powder, dash of chili powder, 1 Tsp. salt. (Blend spices with 3/4 Tbsp. water).

Heat 2 Tsp. of vegetable oil. Add 1Tbsp. butter.

Add the marinated shrimp.

Add a pinch of sugar.

Let cook, stirring often for 4/5 minutes until the marinade starts to give out oil.

Add ½ cup of store-bought coconut milk. Stir well. Cook for about 3 minutes more.

Add salt to taste.

Serve with plain white rice.

Make this dish and make a mom (and children) happy!

"No More Hurting People" May 17, 2013

There is a horrible disconnect here- a devout fanatic prays five times a day with the utmost passion & devotion and then goes out to cause mayhem. Does he truly believe that his God would approve these atrocities towards the innocent? Does he not know that there is nothing, and certainly no one, who can justify crime against humanity? Why is it so hard to understand that you cannot believe in God and worship Satan at the same time?

I don't believe for a minute that there is any God who doubts that Humanity is the only religion. If there is such a God, then I doubt his Godliness.

Whimsical Cobb Salad

1 head Romaine (washed & torn into small pieces)
2 large tomatoes, diced
4 scallions (diagonally cut into thin pieces)
2 ripe Avocados
8 ounces bacon, diced
2 hard cooked eggs, peeled & chopped
2 boneless, skinless chicken breasts (grilled, poached, poached or store-bought)

(A note for my vegetarian friends like Donna Bauman: Please feel free to substitute chicken and bacon for Tofu and other soybean products. Also adding watercress and crunchy red cabbage adds another depth to the salad).

4 ounces Blue cheese, crumbled

Basic vinaigrette:
¼ cup Balsamic Vinegar or regular white wine vinegar
3 Tsp. Dijon Mustard

Juice of 1 lemon
1 Tsp. salt
A pinch of sugar
¾ cups olive oil
Black pepper
Mix everything together and taste away.

Assemble the salad by layering the ingredients and topping off with a generous serving of the vinaigrette. Feel free to toss in any leftovers from the fridge to do justice to how this salad was invented in the first place. Enjoy!

Salute May 24, 2013

The true test of a human being is when one's humanity is put to the test, where there is no scope for rehearsals or retakes and when there is no audience. Today I interrogated myself in the privacy of my own mind: how would I act when catapulted into the most precarious situation where I would have to help a stranger when no one was watching? I shamefully admit that I did not have an answer; truthfully- it seemed most likely that I would try to save myself before anyone else simply because I have too many excuses to live for.

Needless to say, I am truly in awe of what happened that fateful Monday afternoon. The spectators who had gathered to celebrate unsurpassed strength and endurance had no idea that they themselves would be displaying these super-human qualities during the most vulnerable time of their lives. In the midst of the most senseless atrocities, the ordinary people displayed the most extraordinary attributes, which reminded us that there was, after all, light & hope in the darkest and the most hopeless of times.

So here's to all those ordinary people who will never earn a badge of honor or a wreath of victory- know that your heroism was of marathon proportions. You may not have accomplished 26.2 but you certainly achieved **1**.

Mile High Strawberry Pie

1- 9" baked pie shell
10 oz. frozen strawberries
¾ cup sugar
2 egg whites
1 Tbsp. lemon juice
⅛ Tsp. salt

½ cup whipped cream
1 Tsp. vanilla

Place defrosted strawberries, sugar, egg whites, lemon juice and salt in a large mixing bowl. Beat at medium speed for 15 minutes until stiff. Whip the cream and add vanilla. Fold into strawberry mixture. Spoon into the pie shell.

Refrigerate overnight.

Thank you to Aunt Connie for this wonderful recipe! Who doesn't need a little sweetness in their lives?

Distressed Driver May 31, 2013

Driving down the all too familiar road, I caught a glimpse of a police cruiser parked next to a motorcycle, the two officers gravely discussing pressing matters while awaiting the next offender. As I approached them and made eye contact with the burly cop while he exited the vehicle, I was convinced that he was beckoning me to stop.

I pulled over gingerly, rolled my windows down nervously and gathered up the courage to ask sheepishly, "What did I do?" (I was certain that I had done nothing this one time, not even the rebellious 5- mile over the limit driving that I occasionally indulge in). Half smiling-the way only police officers smile-he answered, "Nothing". Empowered by the assurance that I had committed no offence but confused nonetheless, I asked: "Why did you stop me then?" This time he actually smiled and said, "I didn't stop you, *you* stopped yourself." Apparently I have graduated from consciously slowing down upon seeing a cop to unconsciously coming to a complete halt. Quite embarrassing, I must admit, but at least I made two stone-faced officers chuckle.

In honor of Memorial Day, we salute the brave men and women who serve and protect us.

Papa Duke's Seafood Chowder

1-6½ oz. can of minced clams
1-6 oz. can of tiny shrimp
1 medium onion
2 cups of diced potatoes
½ Tsp. salt
1-8 oz. can of cream style corn
1-12 oz. can of evaporated milk

½ Tsp. pepper
⅛ thyme

Drain clams and shrimp; reserve liquid & add water to make one cup.

Melt 1Tsp. butter, add onions and cook till tender.

Add potatoes, reserved liquid and salt.

Cover and cook until potatoes are tender.

Add clams, shrimp, and corn and simmer for about 10 minutes.

Stir in 1 Tbs. of butter, thyme, pepper and heat through but don't boil.

A pot of Mr. Ducott's Chowder would be a heart-warming addition to a sometimes-chilly Memorial Day cookout. Let's count our blessings friends!

Black Ants, White lie June 6, 2013

I love my lying man!

When our little guy asked dad what the ant traps springing up all over the house were for, dad calmly replied, "They will put the ants to sleep" but seeing the sad look on his baby's face, he quickly added "only until next spring". The little guy was clearly relieved that dad was looking out for his black beauties.

A little lie never hurt anyone.

Family Friendly Nacho Plate

1 pound of Ground Beef
½ small onion (chopped)
2 cloves of garlic (chopped)
1 can of Black Beans
1 bag of shredded cheese
Can of jalapenos or Pimientos or Olives according to taste
1 Tbsp. of cumin, Tomato Paste each

Toppings as follows

Start browning Beef in skillet. When halfway through, add the onion & garlic cloves. Mix in cumin & salt/pepper. Add the tomato paste and the olives/jalapenos/pimientos. Set aside.

Add a Tbsp. of oil and drop a can of drained Black Beans and mash with a potato masher or fork. (You may also use a can of Refried Bean instead). Let cook for 3-4 minutes stirring often.

Preheat oven to 350°.

Layer a baking dish with the Beef mixture. Top with a bag of cheddar or Mexican cheese and bake in the oven till cheese starts to melt (about 5 minutes).

On a platter/plate, lay out a generous heaping of tortilla chips; layer the bean and beef mixture and top with scallions, cilantro, sour cream & a healthy dollop of salsa. Enjoy as a meal or a fun appetizer! (I decided to go the healthier route and topped everything but chips over crunchy Romaine). Yummy for moms, dads and hungry kids!

Oh Boy! June 13, 2013

You must have heard about the recent historic ruling- the Boy Scouts of America voted to permit openly homosexual boys as members; the ban against gay adult leaders, however, has not been lifted.

If I may summarize this new ruling—you are allowed to remain a member of the Boy Scouts as long as you are a young, confused gay youth but as soon as you become comfortable in your own skin (& your sexuality), you are deemed doomed. It is then that you will be ousted from the ranks you have achieved through years of persistence even though you clearly imbibe the same core values as your cohorts- embraced through years of dedicated service.

I clearly don't understand the rationale behind the ruling. All I know is that I have met many a gay man with unsurpassed integrity of character and at the same time have had encounters with a few straight men (upstanding community members, if I may add) who have abused innocence. Who are we, with our flawed characters, to judge another human being, simply because he does not confirm to our beliefs? Gay or straight- how does it matter as long as we are civil to each other? Hatred is immoral; we can all rise above it and I certainly think we can teach our boys better.

Roast Beef Panini

Hearty Rolls
2 slices of Roast Beef for each sandwich
1 slice of Swiss cheese for each sandwich
Horseradish spread
Mustard (preferably grainy)
Pickle chips

Spread Mustard on one side and Horseradish on another side of the bread. (This is not the time to be generous). Put a slice of Roast Beef, 3-4 Pickle chips, a second slice of Roast Beef and top off with cheese. (The reason I like to hide the pickle chips in between the meat is so they don't make the bread soggy).

If you own a Panini Maker go for it; if not heat a skillet, butter it just so slightly, place the assembled sandwich over it, put another dab of butter over it and press down with a spatula (or a large can/pot/anything heavy). Make sure the heat is on medium to let the cheese melt and the bread to brown. Enjoy with fries from your Freezer section or a garden salad of Lettuce, tomatoes and cucumbers!

June 20, 2013

Today is my little guy's last day at Preschool. The following article is dedicated to the amazing educators at the Rodman Center Preschool who bring out the best in our little ones. I have no doubt that the world would be a nicer place if everyone was touched by these extraordinary human beings. Their philosophy and practice of patience, caring and acceptance are what we can all draw from to make this world a little sweeter.

Two years ago I dropped off a shy, uncertain 3-year old and today I will be taking home a strong, confident young boy ready to take on the world. How do you thank someone for that?

Dino Stomp

Reading a bedtime story about Dinosaurs to my dino-obsessed preschooler was a humbling experience. Did you know that Dinosaurs roamed the Earth for 18 million years (18,000,000) and lived a whopping 25 million (25,000,000) years ago? We humans have been around the block for only 160,000 years, which means that dinosaurs lived & ruled this earth for 24,840,000 years *before* our grand entrance to "our" planet. The average dinosaur is estimated to have lived between 75 & 300 years whereas if we are lucky we humans live for approximately 72 years. Why then do we act like we are here to stay forever? Why do we assume that our planet is ours to keep? It's hard to imagine a world without me- let alone a world without us. It's hard to think that we are erroneous in our thoughts but in the bigger scheme of things nothing matters but the DINO footprints that we leave behind- so let's get along humans.

Magic Cookies

½ cup butter
2 Tbsp. sugar
1 Tsp. vanilla
1 cup of almonds (finely ground)
1 cup sifted flour
Confectioner's sugar
Heat oven to 300°.
Grease a cookie sheet.

Cream butter & sugar; stir in the vanilla. Stir in the flour to incorporate well and then the nuts.

Roll the dough into small balls (about an inch) and bake for about 30 minutes. Roll the balls while still warm, in Confectioner's sugar. Lightly sweetened, these cookies are truly magical!

Parent Hood June 27, 2013

I threatened to ground my teenager if he did not put his laundry away after repeated requests; he did not- so I followed up on my threat. It was tough love in action. The big boy protested but was powerless and had to give in to mom's rules.

Watching him sitting cross-legged in his room, flipping through pages after pages of Time Magazine, I felt sad but powerful. This was an uncomfortable feeling for I could see in my mind's eyes how some parents could misuse this power.

Happy Summer everyone and may we all make good choices!

Light & Summery Quinoa Salad

1 Pkg. of Quinoa (about a cup) prepared according to directions.
Whisk together ¼ cup freshly squeezed lemon juice
2 Tbsp. of lemon zest
¼ cup extra-virgin olive oil
Salt & pepper to taste

Combine the dressing with the Quinoa and then add the following:

A handful of finely chopped Parsley (or Mint if you like)

1 pint of cherry tomatoes
1 English cucumber
1 small red pepper (veggies should be finely chopped)
1 small can of drained chickpeas

Let sit for a while so that the flavors can combine.

Sprinkle crumbled Feta Cheese before serving!

(Feel free to substitute Quinoa with Couscous or even Bulgur).

The Spy Who Loves Me July 4, 2013

There are reports that the government is spying on us, surveying our phone calls, Facebook and other social media interactions. Many are outraged at the loss of freedom and erosion of our basic rights. All I have to say is that we lost our sense of freedom when evil flew into the Twin Towers that fateful September morning; our sense of carefreeness was blown up when twin evil ransacked our sacred city on a balmy March afternoon.

In an ideal world, I would love to preserve my privacy but these are less than perfect times; we are talking about ruthless terrorism in our daily lives, whether it is another day at work in a skyscraper or a day of doing good downtown. Spying on my "Status" to shield me is a small price to pay. I say bring it on- I have nothing to worry for I have nothing to hide. I'd rather have Big Brother watch my back than have deranged brothers disrupt my life and my loved ones.

Happy Independence Day friends!

Super Easy Coconut Bars

Melt ½ stick of butter. Mix 2 cups of graham cracker crumbs with the melted butter.
Spray a 9x13" rectangular pan with cooking spray.
Spread the crumbs evenly on the bottom of the pan.
Pour 1 can (14 oz.) sweetened condensed milk over the crumbs.
Layer the following:
2 cups of sweetened coconut flakes
1½ cup of chocolate chips (or butterscotch chips or both)
1 cup of Peanut butter cups, m&m's or any other candy that you crave. (I personally love toffee bits and walnuts).

Bake at 350° for approximately 25 minutes. Cut into about 3" bars. I dare you to walk away with just one.

Manhunt July 11, 2013

A happy hubby, a dormant little man, a perfect quiet evening to myself watching a movie after many moons - or so I thought! About 15 minutes into my feel-good chick flick, eight soaking, awkward boys playing "manhunt" in the rain crashed my lovely, lonesome party (and my calm) hunting for food. So much for a perfect start to the summer! Or is this the last vestiges of innocence?

Jill's Buffalo Chicken Sandwiches with Blue Cheese Dressing

Tyson Chicken Strips (Fully cooked- Heat in oven according to directions)

1 bottle of Franks' Red Hot Sauce- (Mild/original/hot)
1 stick of Butter (Drop half the stick if you are trying to drop a few pounds)
Hearty Rolls
Lettuce
Good Blue Cheese Dressing
Melt butter in saucepan.
Add bottle of Franks' Sauce.

Once chicken is heated, pour sauce over chicken & toss to coat well. Remove chicken from sauce with tongs.

Serve on toasted hearty rolls with lettuce & Blue Cheese Dressing.

Yum, Yum, Yum!

UnAmerican July 18, 2013

Sebastian de la Cruz, a 10-year old boy with a gem of a voice, was recently ridiculed on social media sites. His crime: singing the Star Spangled Banner at an NBA game dressed in a Mexican charro outfit. The fact that Sebastian was born and raised in America, and that his father served in the US Navy, were obviously not enough to prevent a nasty racist backlash. The Mariachi suit was apparently too much to bear for those who'd rather be dressed in a glory suit.

The more I hear these buffoons, the more I am convinced that there needs to be a new category of Ethnicity along with the all too obvious ones like Hispanic; I think it should be called Moronic.

Easy Guacamole Fit for a Fiesta

8 ripe Avocados
Juice of 4 lemons
salt to taste
3 ripe tomatoes (seeded so the dip does not get too runny, discard the seeds or add it to your favorite salad)
1 serrano chili pepper (seeded)
½ of a red onion
A handful of cilantro (discard the naked stems on the bottom)
5 cloves of garlic

Chunk avocados and drench with lemon juice to stop from turning brown. Pulse in food processor separately & keep aside. (Use a potato masher if you don't have a food processor).

Pulse tomatoes, chili, onion, cilantro & garlic and then mix everything with avocadoes. Check for and add salt as needed.

Add a Tsp. of cumin powder.

Also add 1 Tsp. of chilly powder if you crave heat. Mix very well to combine the ingredients.

Enjoy with tortilla or Pita chips.

Don't be afraid to try this easy recipe; it will save you a ton of money and earn you a ton of praise!

A Kiss & a Hug July 26, 2013

It is natural for mom to yearn "a hug and a kiss" from her little person. There is nothing in the world sweeter than a big embrace from those little hands and a delicate peck on the lips while on the run. These are the reasons why, I think, we mommies have babies in the first place. My 14- year old is too cool for these random shows of affection these days but it is heart-warming to see him occasionally beg his baby brother for "just one hug & one kiss please". Even though my boys will be boys and they mostly fight like there is no tomorrow, this simple act of "selfless" give and take, gives me plenty of hope for tomorrow.

Divine Fresh Mozzarella Sandwiches

For each sandwich you will need:
Ciabatta Rolls or some kind of hearty bread (Plain old sliced bread will NOT do justice)
3-4 Fresh Mozzarella slices
2-3 thin tomato slices
1-2 Basil leaves--thinly slivered
Pepper Flakes- if you desire heat

Halve the rolls and toast them to medium in the toaster oven.

Take them out and brush them with olive oil (about 1 tbsp. on each side).

Sprinkle the bottom of the roll with a few red pepper flakes (optional) and top with the cheese. Stick it back in the toaster oven till it starts to melt- yummm!!!

Top with the tomatoes and basil. Put the top back on and devour. Divine!!!

Lives Well Lived August 1, 2013

While I was saddened by the shocking news of nineteen young firefighters lost mercilessly, I found comfort in the recurring words of the fallen heroes' grief-stricken relatives: "It brings us peace knowing that he died doing what he loved the most". How selfless and strong does one have to be to look at a tragedy of such epic proportions with such a positive outlook instead of wallowing in self-pity? - I wondered.

This is particularly awe evoking having grown up in an Eastern society where a tragedy, like the unexpected death of a loved one, is an instantaneous death sentence for those still alive. It brought back memories of my mom whose life came to a standstill after my father passed away suddenly. Dad who loved traveling collapsed at the airport without any warning. For years thereafter, there were discussions about how she should not have let him gone and debates about how different things would have been if not for that whirlwind tour. The conclusion was always the same- mom blamed herself for not holding him back, which now that I am older (and a little wiser), translates into- letting him lead the life that he loved.

As much as we would like to believe otherwise, it is an undeniable fact that we are here to stay for only a little while. Why prolong and carry on a series of mundane events that simply turn the wheels of life instead of racing full force ahead doing what we truly love? We are often so focused on leading a "long, safe" life that we forget to enjoy the beauty & fullness of a life well lived, even if it does not conform to our idea of what "full" truly means.

Garret Zuppiger, 27, one of the lives taken by the towering inferno, recently wrote in his blog the simple words- "Everyday is like a gift". Let's enjoy this simple yet uncommon gift that we have been given by living life to the fullest everyday of our lives.

Best Chicken Salad Pitas

1 store bought Rotisserie chicken (skin & bones removed)
½ cup finely chopped celery
2 scallions, finely chopped
1 Tbsp. finely chopped fresh parsley
½ cup Mayonnaise
Juice of 1 lemon
Salt & Pepper
Pita bread

Chop the chicken finely and mix it with the above ingredients. Open the pockets and stuff with a generous helping of the salad. Top off with Romaine lettuce.

Friends Aug 8, 2013

The following recipe comes from my friend Karen Feeney. Karen & I met at a birthday party for preschoolers. It was one of those occasions where you have to stand around with a pretty smile—disguising the discomfort of making small talk with complete strangers, brought together by rambunctious little people.

We hit it off right away; we talked about a million things that evening, none of which I remember today. All I remember is that I felt like I had known my newfound friend forever and that there was no stress to impress.

Driving back home, I had a giddy feeling just like my little preschooler returning from his delightful adventure with his little pals. Somehow I knew that Karen & I would become good friends some day. Fortunately (even though I am not right very often for I happen to run on emotions and not everyone shares my emotional highs), I was pretty accurate this one time.

The other night, before going to bed, my little guy matter-of-factly declared to me: "Mom, do you know that Jack & I loved each other the minute we saw each other?" I assured him that I knew exactly what he meant because "Jack's mom and I liked each other the minute we saw each other". I was secretly elated that this mutual admiration transcended age and traversed generations. Here's to friendship that never discriminates!

Karen's Easy Fish Dish

4-7oz. Cod/Haddock steaks
1 Tsp. dried Oregano
Salt and freshly ground pepper to taste

⅛ Tsp. cayenne Pepper
6 ripe plum tomatoes (cut into ½" thick slices)
1 Tsp. olive oil
1 Tsp. minced garlic
Parsley
Sprinkle fish with spices, salt & pepper.
Salt & pepper tomatoes.

Heat oil in large skillet.

Cook fish about 4-5 minutes on each side.

Add tomatoes and garlic when you flip fish.

Simmer until fish feels firm but slightly flaky.

(Makes 4 servings for 4 good friends).

All in a Day's News August 15, 2013

This is what was on just about every news channel the same otherwise ordinary morning:

Congressman Anthony Weiner announced that he had "continued to engage in inappropriate relationships with, 6 to 10 women, I suppose". This is after resigning from Congress in disgrace and soon thereafter declaring that he had been reformed.

Lance Armstrong accused the Postal Service- the organization that had sponsored him for years, of knowing that he was abusing drugs all those years and therefore, this was their fault. This is after years of doping, lying and denying.

Edward Snowden's dad slammed "those who would focus on the sinner rather than the sins" and stated "the Government's zeal to torture his son unconscionable". This came after his son leaked top-secret Government surveillance programs compromising the safety of millions of Americans.

San Diego Mayor Bob Filner promised to come back "the best Mayor I can be" before leaving for two weeks of intensive therapy to improve his behavior towards women. This is after being accused of gross sexual misconduct towards dozens of women while on his job. (I cannot help but mention that this announcement came just as the Mayor was preparing to be the keynote speaker at an event on military sexual assault towards women veterans)!

As parents and educators, we teach and expect our children to take responsibility for their actions; why then, are these powerful men, seeking to shift the blame, making a mockery of their morals and their manhood? Truthfully I think my little guy, even at his tender age, has better judgment than these shaky pillars of society that he is supposed to look up to.

Aunt Connie's Golden Brownie Chip Bars

2¼ cups flour
2½Tsp. baking powder
¾ cup butter or margarine
1¼ cups sugar
1¼ cups light brown sugar
1 Tsp. vanilla
3 eggs
12 oz. chocolate chips

Preheat oven to 350°.

In a large bowl, beat the butter, brown sugar and vanilla until creamy. Add the eggs one at a time beating well after each addition. Mix the flour, baking powder and salt; then gradually stir into the creamed mixture. Stir in the chocolate chips.

Spread evenly in a greased 15X10X1" jelly roll pan.

Bake at 350° for 35 to 40 minutes. Cool and cut into squares.

Past- the best present Aug. 22, 2013

China just passed a new law; it allows adult children, who do not visit their elderly parents, to be sued. This law is well meaning — meant to protect aging parents neglected by their offspring but how sad is it that the Government has to step in to teach children to love their parents again?

Respect for the elderly, a trait that was ingrained in the Chinese psyche ever since the beginning of civilization, is apparently being drained by reforms in these modern times. Modern-day advances responsible for deterioration of moral responsibilities- now that's a concept!

This is not just a Chinese problem but a problem, often in our own backyards.

When a value as basic as respecting and taking care of those responsible for making us who we are, wanes, so does the soul of a society. If the past has no value, what worth does the future have?

It may be cool to break away from the past but let's remember that a branch that breaks away from its roots will eventually wither away. In honor of National Senior Citizen's Day celebrated around the country only yesterday, let's pledge to be kind to each other, especially to those who need us today just like we needed them once.

My Mom's Easy Leftover Fried Rice

1 cup of mixed frozen vegetables microwaved in a covered container for about 3 minutes or 1 cup of chopped fresh veggies- carrots, peppers, cauliflower, peas etc.

2 cups of rice- cooked, drained and kept aside when still slightly hard to the touch.

Leftover cooked meat of your choice for e.g. chicken, pork, steak pieces, ham or shrimp.

Heat pan and add a Tbsp. of oil; add frozen or fresh veggies. Sauté till color starts to change. Keep aside. Put another Tsp. of oil and add the following:

1 Tbsp. of soy sauce

1 Tsp. of ketchup

1 Tsp. cornstarch- mixed with a little water.

Stir constantly and let reduce. Add veggies, salt to taste, and the rice. Stir well until well mixed. Garnish with scallions and chopped, boiled eggs (optional).

Hustle and "Bus"tle August 29, 2013

The all too familiar sights of a new school year never cease to amaze me. My eyes well up every time I see a crossing guard stopping traffic to let little boys and girls walk; my heart cries a little every time the blinking stop sign of a school bus, halting to pick-up or a drop-off just another child, brings to a standstill the traffic on all sides. There is something so pure, so unselfish and so innocent about this simple act of letting others ahead of you, no matter how important you are or how important your mission is. If only we could all be a little more kindly and occasionally put others ahead of us even in the rush hours of life, this world would be a more serene place even if only for a minute.

Here's to all the wonderful people who make the wonder happen! May all of us have a remarkable school year!

Chicken Marsala

4 skinless, boneless, chicken breasts (about 1½ pounds)
Kosher salt and freshly ground black pepper
¼ cup extra-virgin olive oil
4 ounces prosciutto, thinly sliced
8 ounces mushrooms, stemmed and halved
½ cup sweet Marsala wine
½ cup chicken stock
2 tablespoon unsalted butter
¼ cup chopped flat-leaf parsley
Season chicken with salt & pepper.

Heat the oil in a large skillet. When the oil is hot, dredge both sides of the chicken cutlets in the seasoned flour, shaking off the excess. Slip the cutlets into the pan when hot and fry well on each side until golden, turning once. Remove the chicken to a large platter in a single layer to keep warm.

Lower the heat to medium and add the prosciutto to the drippings in the pan, sauté for 1 minute to render out some of the fat. Now, add the mushrooms and sauté until they are nicely browned and their moisture has evaporated, about 5 minutes; season with salt and pepper. Pour the Marsala in the pan and boil down for a few seconds to cook out the alcohol. Add the chicken stock and simmer for a minute to reduce the sauce slightly. Stir in the butter and return the chicken to the pan; simmer gently for 1 minute to heat the chicken through. Season with salt and pepper and garnish with chopped parsley before serving.

Serve with your favorite pasta or egg noodles.

Thank You Sept 5, 2013

"Piglet sidled up to Pooh from behind. "Pooh?" he whispered.

"Yes, Piglet?"

"Nothing," said Piglet, taking Pooh's hand. "I just wanted to be sure of you."

— A.A. Milne, *Winnie-the-Pooh*

September is here which means that it has been a year since you welcomed me into your hearts and homes.

Today I thought I should take a minute to thank each of you for your support. I have met many wonderful people thanks to the column; some of you I have gotten to know well for the very first time, some deeper than ever before, others I have met in passing, and many more of you have become my Thursday afternoon confidants. These interactions—of every shape and form—mean the world to me and I am truly grateful. And even though we may not always see eye to eye, I do mean it when I say that it has been a pleasure writing for you.

Take care my friend and see you next Thursday....

Pork/Leftover Surprise Sandwich

For each sandwich you will need:

Leftover meat, thinly sliced, about 4/5 small pieces. (I find store-marinated pork loin meant for a slow cooker, an awesome buy in terms of saving time & money).

1 Hearty Ciabatta Roll

A slice of Salsa Jack or Pepper Jack cheese

A few of slices of Roasted Red Peppers from a jar (pat dried on a paper towel)

2-3 thinly sliced red onions

3-4 torn Romaine lettuce leaves

Toast the bread halfway. Put the cheese slice on the top roll and put Rolls back separately in toaster oven for a few minutes or until the cheese starts to melt.

Put a Tsp. each of Mayonnaise and Dijon Mustard on the bottom roll and start assembling the sandwich with lettuce, meat, red peppers and onions. Put the top back on & enjoy but beware- these can be highly addictive!

Of Dungeons and Dudes September 12, 2013

As we were getting ready to move to our house some eleven years ago, my little guy was reluctant to give up the only place familiar to him. In an attempt to get him excited, I bribed him with the little room in the basement and told him that some day he could have this "secret" room all to himself. This shot to make him want to move, backfired miserably; the toddler cried and clung to me. I realized how terrified he was of the little room and the prospect of having to somehow leave his mother. He made me promise that I would never make him go there and I gladly complied.

This past weekend, my now not so little boy moved himself into the dungeon. As I reminded him of the promise, he laughed heartily and said he couldn't believe how "stupid" he was. His little brother, who did not see any humor in all of this, assured me that unlike "bro", he would *never ever* move and that he will stay with me *forever*. I teared up and wanted to tell him that "forever" is too short-lived but decided to keep the childish innocence and the unwavering loyalty to mom unscathed for now.

Miss Alicia's Super Easy Steak & Cheese Egg Rolls

1 package of Shaved Steak (from the fresh meat section, about a Pound)

American Cheese (12 slices), sliced in halves

Wonton/Egg Roll Wraps (package of approximately 24-available in the produce section)

Vegetable oil for deep-frying

Cook steak on stovetop (takes about a minute) and let cool a bit. Take a wonton wrap and put about 1 Tbsp. of steak shavings and half a piece of cheese in the middle. Wrap as show on the wrap package. Fry until golden brown. Drain on paper towel. I dare you to stop at one!

Thank you, Miss Alicia, for your priceless help in the kitchen and in the classroom.

Gross Inequality Sept 19, 2013

Men & women are created unequal.

Why else is my man able to exit the store- packed with precious finds- with just ONE bath towel that he ventured in for? How cum the treasures do not scream out his name like they do mine? How cum the bejeweled beauties do not make it home with him?

Why is it that he can walk into Shop & Save and walk out with just one Maki Roll? Why isn't he escorting a freshly baked bread that will make its way (yet again) into the freezer? And the most confusing trait of all- how cum a trip to the store for him is over in just under 6 minutes whereas mine has at least a 0 at the end? The speed with which he can walk in and out of a store is vexing and honestly, bothersome. I say ladies- we have been blessed with many things including the gift to enjoy the beauty of our surroundings and the power to surround us with beauty. And for all other practical purposes we have been blessed with our men…

Quick and Yummy Cole Slaw

Ingredients:

1 large bag of shredded coleslaw vegetables
1 cup of mayonnaise
⅓ cup sugar
¼ cup apple cider vinegar
¼ teaspoon celery seed
¼ teaspoon ground black pepper to taste
Salt to taste

Directions:

Combine all ingredients for the dressing (last six.) Whisk together. Taste and adjust seasonings, adding salt and pepper to taste or more mayonnaise and a bit more vinegar if too sweet for your taste. Add dressing to the shredded vegetables in a large bowl. Mix until well moistened. Refrigerate to chill thoroughly. Makes 6-8 side servings.

Thank you to Kate Healey for sharing this recipe. We wish her luck as she joins the staff of Canton High!

Mary Sept 26, 2013

One of my all-time favorite appetizers is the following Bruschetta recipe shared by Mary Laporte. Mary was a wonderful Teaching Assistant I had the pleasure to work with many years ago.

Mary had hauntingly kind eyes and the kindest heart—even though she'd had more than her fair share of sorrow. I often looked at her and wondered how she was never bitter in spite of some very unfortunate events that life had handed her.

Mary is the type of person whom, in this craziness called life, we occasionally have the fortune of meeting- someone who channels her sorrow into something incredibly positive after facing unbelievable adversity. Her mission was to treat everyone around her, even those who were not the nicest to her, with utmost kindness, respect and genuine caring. And when I, with my limited patience, told her on more than one occasion that she needs to stop being so nice, her shy answer was, "Oh it's ok, I don't mind." And I can honestly say that Mary didn't mind because she was not capable of seeing the "badness" in anyone.

Over the years I have lost touch with Mary but she is someone I will always remember as a picture of compassion, faith and grace.

I have made this appetizer more than any other starter and with every compliment I have received even in the craziest of times, I have delved into a quiet place in my mind to fondly think about Mary and her kind eyes...

Mary's Bruschetta

½ cup of Mayo
1 cup of Mozzarella cheese
2-diced tomatoes
2 Tbsp. Parmesan cheese
1Tsp. oregano
¼ Tspn. basil
1 clove minced garlic
1 baguette

Mix everything together. Spread butter on bottom of each slice of baguette facing the sheet pan. Spoon mixture onto slices and bake for 15 minutes at 350°. Enjoy!

Welcome to My World! October 3, 2013

Just before school started, we, the proud Kindergarten parents, were graciously invited to meet with the classroom teachers. Hoping to create a good first impression, I had paid particular attention to my outfit and accessories. I walked in confidently just in time to see Mrs. F. greeting each parent with a firm handshake while exchanging pleasantries. As she reached out to me in front of the packed auditorium, my dangling bracelets got stuck to the back of my crocheted shirt. As I quickly tried to free the right hand with the left, the watch caught the bracelet which in turn left me locked in a handcuffed position- both hands tied to my back while a very confused Mrs. F. stood there staring at me with her extended hand. Finally when I was able to explain to her my dire predicament (both my hands having miraculously disappeared), she did extricate me from the shackles much to the dismay of the other parents who did not see anything except what appeared to be a very recalcitrant and discombobulated me. And when I thanked her profusely and assured her (in the loudest voice possible) that this is not something that happens to me ordinarily, she smiled quite artificially.

The next time when I saw Mrs. F. just as my right foot clumsily tripped my left, while casually walking into the school office, I noticed she did not reach out to me with her outstretched hand…

Last Minute Grilled Salmon

2 Pounds Salmon Fillet
2 cloves of finely chopped garlic
2 Tbsp. soy sauce
1 Tbsp. Worcestershire sauce
1 Tsp. pepper
Mix ingredients 2-5.

Marinate fish in the above sauce for at least 15 minutes.

Grill fish about 4 minutes on each side (a small indoor grill works well but remember to spray generously with cooking spray).

Served with wild rice and stir-fry veggies. I used a combination of zucchini, red peppers, green beans and sautéed them with garlic and a Tbsp. of olive oil, salt & pepper.

***Look for an easy and delicious veggie wrap with the leftover sautéed veggies in next week's column.

"We" the People... October 10, 2013

Who doesn't like Dr. Seuss? But do you think you or I could get away with reciting "Green Eggs and Ham" at work? How about rambling for hours— 21.9 to be precise, without stopping, to make a point? How about slamming the boss, calling her despicable names (in public) and then, refusing to work, which not only impacts my family, but the families of millions? How come a not-so-genteel phone call greets me if I forget to pay for a $1.00 Heath bar charged to my MasterCard? Why am I slapped with a $25.00 late fee for sending in my $15.00 Amex bill just a day late? Disgraceful name-calling, an ugly blame game and a childish meltdown leading to a shutdown of the Government — how are these acceptable?

We, the ordinary folks, are expected to do our jobs with no drama and pay our bills without any fuss day in and day out, so why are these guys who represent us (and make a not-so-shabby base salary of $174,000), allowed to indulge in such histrionics? Can you imagine having a tantrum at work just because you don't agree with the boss lady? Not only do I shudder to think about its implications, I also believe that most of us would never partake in such unprofessional and unethical behavior simply because it is wrong.

How ironic is this drama when "we" (they) are the ones called upon to solve the world's most pressing problems? Anytime there is a conflict anywhere— even in the farthest reaches of the world— "we" (they) are expected to forge ahead and settle these differences judiciously. Quite bizarre—wouldn't you agree?

I say let's introspect people— charity begins in the HOUSE!

Veggie Wrap

3 whole-wheat tortillas
Shredded cheese of any kind
1 zucchini (cut lengthwise, about 2" thick and 6" long)
1 red pepper
1 red onion (sliced)
a few green beans, trimmed and halved
1 clove of garlic, minced
In a Tbsp. of olive oil, sauté garlic and onions.

Add green beans and sauté for about 4 minutes on medium heat. Add the rest of the veggies and any fresh herbs you like and cook on high heat for another 3-4 minutes stirring often. Sprinkle with salt & pepper (and pepper flakes if you are like me). The point is to keep the veggies crunchy and somewhat charred and not turn them mushy or burnt.

In a pan, heat a wrap for 30 seconds on one side. Fold it in half and stuff in veggies generously sprinkling cheese especially around the edges so that the cheese acts as a sealant. Let the cheese melt by cooking the tortilla for another minute.

(Last week, I brought this wrap to work every single day; yet I must admit I never tired of it and actually craved more while feeling good about what I was eating). Try it- I promise you will get hooked.

Remember October 17, 2013

Many years ago I had the fortune of meeting Dr. G.

A brief stint at housesitting turned into a priceless relationship that lasted many years. Soon after the first encounter, my husband and I-both starving students at the time, moved into the in-law apartment of her sprawling estate where we lived for almost 10 years.

Dr. G was a brilliant Psychoanalyst, who read minds beautifully. She was completely self-made— a milliner's daughter and the first of her migrant family to attend college at a time when it was not common for women to attend Harvard Medical School. Her wit and wisdom were unmatched and to this day she remains one of the most broad-minded and genuinely smart people I have met.

It was a time when I myself was starting life as a young woman having just moved thousands of miles away from home (and mom). Mrs. G. gave me invaluable, common sense advise on everything from relationships to authentic Yiddish cuisine. She was the one to admonish me and tell me that "It is okay to say no" when she saw me frazzled one afternoon trying to cook & clean for guests in spite of being just tired.

Dr. G. became my surrogate mother; we celebrated many landmarks together- her 75th birthday, our graduations, the birth of my first son, moving her mother to an assisted facility when her Alzheimer's worsened, and occasions too many to mention but those that have left an indelible mark on me- like running up to her to share my very first homemade Mandelbrot.

We eventually moved out of Dr. G's house to our own and for the next ten years I continued to deeply miss those priceless moments.

You may have inferred by now that Dr. G. was an exceptionally wealthy woman. She was very generous, donating to many charities and helping those in need; yet she led a simple life, cutting coupons and traveling the world on economy class.

Do you know what her money is doing now? Her well-earned savings are funding a staff of helpers who take care of her because she can no longer do so herself. Her memory has failed and she is patiently waiting to be moved into a Senior Care Facility, where she will be seen as another quirky, difficult and stubborn old lady—just the way I saw her mother. If only they knew her, the way I knew her….

Dr. G.'s Sirloin Pork Roast

Pork Loin, about 3 Pounds—make deep incisions on Pork sides. Marinate Pork Sirloin (about 3 Lbs.) in a mixture of 1 Tbsp. Soy sauce, crushed garlic cloves (6-8) and ginger (½Tsp. fresh or ground) for a day. Rub kosher salt (½ Tsp.) & pepper; coat with a handful of fresh rosemary leaves and paprika (½ Tsp.).

Roast Pork on a rack placed on a roasting pan at 350° preheated oven for approximately 60-75 minutes or until internal temperature reaches 145°F on a meat thermometer (new USDA recommendation).

Good God! October 24, 2013

My little guy was visibly perplexed when I added "God" to his list of "Things We Can't Talk About in School" along with guns, shooting and bad guys. Confused, he asked, "Why can't we talk about God- I thought he was a good guy? How the heck was I supposed to explain to a pure-hearted 4-year old that often, the world that he lives in acts more immaturely than him?

Homemade Reese's Peanut Butter Candy

Thanks to Jill for sharing another one of Aunt Connie's super hit recipes! Perhaps you will try this kid-friendly recipe for Halloween. May Aunt Connie's sweet soul rest in peace!

1 cup Peanut Butter
1⅓ sticks butter or Margarine melted
3 cups Graham Cracker crumbs
1⅓ cups Confectioners sugar
12 oz. pkg. chocolate bits
1 can sweetened condensed milk⅓

Mix the peanut butter, butter or margarine, Graham Cracker crumbs and sugar together. Pat into a 13x9" pan. The mixture will be stiff.

Over very low heat, melt the chocolate chips in the condensed milk. While hot, spread over the peanut butter mixture.

Refrigerate at least 30 minutes. Cut into small squares and enjoy!

Dirty Driver October 30, 2013

I was minding my own business waiting to take a left turn at the lights when suddenly my eyes were drawn to the cars next to me. The 2 vehicles were waiting to take a right and the car in the back, a little impatient with the first car standing still, sounded a gentle horn to remind the driver that the coast was clear. No sooner did the horn toot that the driver in front responded by holding up his middle finger with the ease of a well-choreographed & perfectly timed dance move. It was almost like this testy driver was holding his finger in position waiting to stick it up. That was impressive; I could never do anything like that— I thought! It would take me a good minute to locate my middle finger, position the rest in place and then aim it at someone. I truly think that my coordination skills are severely compromised; no wonder I can never curse anyone with crude gestures- only occasional an under-the-breath "stupid" or if I am way too agitated- perhaps an "idiot". But the more I thought, the more I concluded that I'd rather be slow and steady than nimble and nasty…

On this fun-filled, kid-friendly day, let's vow to be a little more patient than usual!

Bloody Good Barbequed Franks—
an Easy Halloween Dinner

1 medium onion chopped
1 tbsp. sugar
salt & pepper to taste
½ cup water
12 Franks
3 tbsp. salad oil
1 Tsp. paprika
½ cup ketchup
¼ cup vinegar

Cook inions in the oil till tender. Add all ingredients except the Franks. Simmer for 10 minutes. Make a long slice in the center of each frank. Cover with the sauce.

Bake at 375° for 30 minutes. Baste often.

Enjoy over toasted buns.

November 7, 2013

Another Thanksgiving is around the corner and this year I have decided to stick to the true meaning of this selfless holiday. For the next four weeks I will feature the ordinary people who have made a great impact on the life of others, including mine.

I want to start out by thanking a very special man, Dr. Gerald Fain, to whom I will be eternally grateful for making me who I am today.

Dean Fain

Well, I must admit that I have never done things traditionally— mainly because I have no patience. So when it came to following my dreams to be an educator, I embarked on a rather unconventional route.

One day I found my heart set on Boston University and without further ado, I decided to walk into the Dean's office (yes- what was I thinking?). That's when I met Dr. Fain. At first I was quite daunted by the fiery redhead with a serious countenance and a no-bull attitude. I began to nervously question my rash decision to approach him in this manner but as we started talking I realized that he was a genuine human being and a passionate believer in children. He asked me a million straightforward questions, which I answered honestly; I also told him that I was penniless yet my dreams, though modest, were big. All I wanted to do was teach kids with disabilities and give them a fair shot at life. Soon I realized that a brilliant educator and an ordinary girl from another world had a lot in common and so we talked effortlessly for over an hour, sharing our strangely common experiences but most of all— a human bond.

It was only a month later that I received a letter from the Dean's Office stating that I had been accepted into the Master's program— all expenses paid. The enormity of the decision that rested upon one compassionate man had only just begun to hit me.

It has been many years since that first (and final) meeting with Dr. Fain but I often think about the faith he bestowed upon a complete stranger.

Thank you Dr. Fain for your trust in me, and inspiring me to pay it forward! It is people like Dr. Fain who help make this world a better place—one person at a time.

Patty's Apple Pie

8 apples sliced
¾ cup of sugar (may use substitute sugar)
2 tbsp. flour
1tsp. cinnamon
Dash of nutmeg
1 pkg. of 2 deep-dish pie shells (frozen)

Mix sugar, flour and spices together; sprinkle & mix with apples in bowl.

Add to pie shell.

Dot with butter.

Cover with remaining pie shell.

Use milk on the pie shell to seal and on top to brown.

Poke a few holes with a fork.

Cover with aluminum foil so crust isn't done before pie. Bake at 400° for a total of 50 minutes (with foil on for the first 20 minutes and off for the next 30 minutes).

Thank you to Pat Falcione for this easy recipe! Also, best wishes to dear Patty for a quick recovery so many more delicious pies can be made and had!

Ms. K. November 14, 2013

The following recipe comes from a co-worker's brother-in-law's grandmother—Lou Harrell, lovingly known as Mama Lou. May I take this opportunity to thank my co-worker for passing this recipe to me? Better still, may I also take this opportunity to thank Ms. Killian for who she is?

Ms. K. is essentially the teacher who Forest Witcraft had in mind when he wrote his famous quote 63 years ago. Time and again, Ms. K. has been there for that student who desperately needed a real-life superhero. In this age of rigid protocols and "doing everything by the book", Ms. K. is quite the rebel. She understands well that a student who is hurting inside cannot be superficially groomed but needs to be educated— inside out. Many of her weekends are spent shopping and cooking for students and their families who cannot afford luxuries or bare necessities, and at games cheering kids whose families do not have the time to do so. This selfless giving of precious time is, to me, the greatest gift one can give a troubled child. In fact, I shamefully admit that recently we were at a party on a beautiful fall weekend where food, wine & good times flowed freely; Ms. K. stayed for just under an hour as she had a commitment to attend a student's Football Game while I myself kept indulging in the good times though my own son was at that same game! (It worked out great for me; Ms. K. gave my son a ride to the game!)

Of course there are always those who will complain about others doing too much (and doing too little and everything in between); in fact, I too may have callously commented that "Ms. K. needs to get a life" clearly forgetting that many of our kids' real lives begin when that closing bell rings.

I say that we need more teachers like Ms. K. to educate our kids and adults like me about the power we (can) wield in the life of another. And honestly, if ever my own child were drifting, I would like him to find someone like Ms. K. to steer him right. You see— we often forget that school is not just for high achievers with their perfect lives, but for under achievers as well, with less than perfect lives. Thank you to teachers like Ms. K. who take this oath of "educating all our children" to heart without any claim to fame and who are always ready to take the plunge to save another lost soul.

There is no bigger achievement than leaving this world a bit nicer than how we found it. On second thought, teaching the next generation to do the same is an even greater achievement. Kudos to the ordinary teachers like Ms. K. for achieving both so effortlessly!

Overnight Potato Rolls (makes 30- 3" rolls)

In a large bowl, dissolve 1 package of dry yeast and 1 Tsp. sugar in 1½ cups warm water. Add 1¼ Tsp. salt, ⅔ cup sugar, ⅔ cup shortening, 1 cup of mashed potatoes, and 2 slightly beaten eggs, stirring until well blended. Add 3½ cups of flour, stirring until smooth. Gradually add another 3½ cups of flour, stirring after each addition.

Knead dough on a lightly floured board for 3-5 minutes.

Return dough to large bowl, covering loosely with plastic wrap to allow expansion.

Refrigerate dough for 12-24 hours.

Punch down dough.

Roll out dough on lightly floured board to ¾" thickness. Cut out rolls and place on baking sheet. Cover and let rise for 2 hours. Bake at 400° for 10-13 minutes or until light golden brown.

Hero with a Heart November 21, 2013

One afternoon my life came to a temporary standstill to watch the superstar with the million-dollar smile (and the million dollar perks). Thank God for Talk Shows! Surely the world could wait for an hour while I devoured every word Mr. Right had to say. I wanted to hear him pour his heart out on love, life, and his recipe for success. After all, he was the new star of a million dollar blockbuster that had captivated all of America! What a hero, what an inspiration-I and a million others like me, mused! But slowly as the big-screen hero (and his fame) began to fade as quickly as he had appeared, it occurred to me that the real hero was not the overrated, overpaid, over-handsome young actor but the underpaid, underrated, middle-aged, ordinary cop who had come to my classroom the same day that my life would temporarily come to a halt. Officer McCormack had taken an hour of his busy day of helping those in need to talk to a room full of kids—to answer their pure-hearted queries about "bad guys and guns". No applause, no million dollar bonus, no press, no perks, no nothing-only pure heroism.

In honor of Thanksgiving, please join me in thanking those countless, selfless, unseen heroes who tirelessly work behind the scenes to protect us.

Pat's Potatoes

2 lb. frozen hash browns, thawed	1 can cream of celery soup
½ cup butter	½ teaspoon pepper
8 oz. sour cream	1 cup shredded cheddar cheese (for top)

Mix the first five ingredients together well and place in a 9 x 13 x 2 inch casserole. Top with cheese. Bake for 1-½ hours at 350°F.

Cover with aluminum foil if cheese on top is getting too brown. This dish is great with a baked ham or with a Sunday brunch or for planning ahead for the next big holiday!

Thank you to Kate Healey for sharing another one of mom's wonderful recipes!

The Final Thank You November 28, 2013

I was all set to start writing my final article for November about being thankful for Nurse Betty when something happened. As I sat there on my computer finishing up my thoughts, I got sick—really, really sick. It was a mega migraine that came out of nowhere and left me completely incapacitated. It was a helpless feeling, my husband being eight thousand miles away and my teenager, fast asleep in his dungeon. I picked up the phone and tried calling him to take care of his little brother but try awakening a demon that was up all night conquering and fighting his way through cyber space! I was distraught but tried not to upset my little guy too much. I explained to him that I needed to rest and sent him off to watch T.V. But this made things worse because the noise down the hall sounded like death pounding on my head. That is when I decided to take a long hot shower hoping to wash away whatever had taken hold of my body. After a few minutes, I heard a faint knock on the door. It was the little guy checking on mom and genuinely wondering if she was "dead". I must shamefully admit that, still under the spell of whatever had possessed me, I yelled an unkind word or two which may have sounded like this: "I wish I was dead because you guys can't give me two minutes of peace". It turned quite peaceful after that, the peace finally punctured by the pitter-patter of scurrying feet. As I emerged, half sick, half mad and half curious, I was greeted by Dolphy, Teddy & Ele and a drawing left outside the bathroom door that said "I *lik* mom. I *hop* mom is not *ded*". The picture (as he translated it for me) was that of a sickly woman (mom) with a sword fighting a deadly pirate (germs). As I gave him a hug, he asked again, innocently, "Mom, will you die today?" I promised him, I will not— not today, not tomorrow, not ever because his love will always keep me alive.

(And when my Sleeping Beast finally awoke from his slumber, he informed me in his rather concerned voice that "there is a Brain Eating Amoeba going around, the first signs of which is a massive headache, followed by a stomach ache and you have exactly two weeks before you die unless you see the doctor right away")....

So here is the final **Thank You** to all the blessings in our life (however small or big) that make us want to live forever!

Simple Salsa Meatloaf

1lb ground Turkey
¾ jar of salsa
¾ cup instant oats
Low fat Cheddar cheese

Preheat oven to 375°.

Mix everything together and put in a loaf pan.

Cook for 50 minutes.

Take out of the oven and top with cheddar cheese (do as much as you want...less if you are watching what you eat).

Put back in the oven for 10 minutes or until browned to your liking.

Thank you to Mrs. Melissa Johnson for sharing this easy recipe (& her classroom) with me! **Happy Thanksgiving friends!**

Matthew December 5, 2013

The next two recipes come from Matt— my girlfriend Julie's husband. Matt is the kind of guy you want to have on your side. He is sweet, kind, courteous, generous and always incredibly helpful (actually, just about any adjective that is extraordinarily positive applies to Matt).

Four summers ago, Matt and Julie joined us for a trip to India; we did a lot of traveling— exploring new places and savoring different food. Matt kept my kids entertained and was always ready with a smile, carrying the toddler perched in the stroller up & down cumbersome stairs without ever being asked. Everyone who met Matt—from friends & family to complete strangers—had the most wonderful things to say about this young man who won everyone's heart in a strange land. Most of all they commented on what must have been a wonderful upbringing, crediting his parents with raising him well.

I secretly smiled, and until today have never shared with anyone that Matt is who he is because of a relentless resolve to be nothing like those who raised him. You see—Matt had a traumatic childhood, growing up in a house with substance abuse where the adults acted irresponsibly and where he had to quickly take on the role of the caregiver—cooking, cleaning & taking care of himself, his little sister and his parents. And when things couldn't get any worse, mom started turning blind as Matt was entering high school and that was when the drinking became even more rampant. Dad did not know what to do and therefore did nothing.

At eighteen Matt left home, determined to end the cycle of hopelessness and to etch out a better future. He supported himself through college by driving ambulances in Philadelphia. He managed to balance a hectic work schedule with being in the Honors program in college and graduating in just three years.

Today Matt, who himself has no childhood memories, except of emergencies involving his mother, is well on his way to creating a magical childhood for his young son. He is an amazing dad although he does not have personal examples to draw from; he is a loyal husband although all he witnessed growing up was dissension. And mom, whose vision continues to fail in every way even to this day, has moved in with Matt and his young family where she is treated with respect and fairness.

How *does* one set aside the bitter experiences of a lost childhood to the point that he is able to forgive and forget? At 31, Matt has managed to do just that; there is no negativity, just the most incredible positive attitude towards life and a dogged determination to climb every steep step while helping others along the way. To me, this is the true Gospel of Matthew.

Matt's Quick, Zesty Tomato Sauce

1 onion
1 can of San Marzano Tomatoes
½ Lb. Bacon
1 Tsp. sugar
Pinch of Red Pepper Flakes

Sauté bacon until slightly crisp; remove from pan all but 2 Tbsp. of oil.

Heat oil; add chili flakes, followed by chopped onions.

Cook until onions are soft, add tomatoes, then add bacon back in with sugar and boil down to reduce sauce. Makes a quick, easy and special sauce to go over pasta on a hurried night like today.

Say what? December 12, 2013

"*On my way to work, please kill me*"— read the bumper sticker on the car in front of me. Although I should have probably turned a blind eye, I must say that this public expression of frustration bothered me, which probably was the driver's intent. And although I am not one to judge someone I don't know, I do have strong opinions about those who publicly display their personal hatred, anger, or plain old resentment. Don't we all teach our children to practice restraint and treat everyone around them with kindness and dignity? And if this is someone's brilliant way of drawing attention to his pitiful self, I must say that it is just that—pretty pathetic.

I see no humor in public display of deprecation whether it is that of a young man sporting a belittling T-shirt or a grown adult parading a derisive decal. I support the Right to Free Speech but must say that abusing this fundamental right is fundamentally wrong.

Matt Stoltz's Old Fashioned Fruitcake

A Stoltz Family Derivation from 1961 Betty Crocker Cookbook after much experimentation and trial.

I Cup Vegetable Oil
1-⅓ Cups Sugar blend of White and Brown Sugar
4 Eggs
¼ Cup Molasses
2 Cups Flour
1 Tsp. Baking Powder
2 Tsp. Kosher Salt
2 Tsp. Cinnamon
1 Tsp. Nutmeg
1-½ Cups Orange Juice
1 Additional Cup Flour

7-½ Cups Dried Chopped Fruits (NO CANDIED FRUIT--Raisins, Currants, Dates, Pineapple, Apricots are our preferred blend)

1 Cup Walnuts or Pecans (Pecans are sweeter, walnuts are earthier)

Preheat oven to 275°. Take out either 3 full sized or 6 mini loaf pans and line with wax paper. Mix oil, sugars, eggs and molasses and whip for 2 minutes with a spoon or mixer. In a separate bowl, mix flour, baking powder, salt, and spices together. Stir the dry flour mixture into the wet mixture, alternating the dry ingredients with portions of the orange juice as you add it to the wet mixture. Mix the additional cup of flour into the mix of fruit and nuts--this prevents clumping, and allows for even distribution of fruit (DO NOT SKIP THIS STEP!!!!) Mix the batter and the floured fruit together--the fruit and nut mixture will be lightly covered with batter. Pour into loaf pans, fill to near top--cake does not rise much. The full sized loaves will bake 2-3 hours, mini loaves will bake 1 hour. Bake longer if you like a drier cake. Baked cakes will have a heavy, dense consistency, dried fruit cemented together by batter. A toothpick stuck into the center should come out clean. Once removed from oven, allow to sit 15 minutes before removing cake from the pan. Allow to cool completely on a cooling rack. From here they are edible, but better if allowed to sit, wrapped tightly in 2 layers of tinfoil and stored in a cool, dry place. After being cut into, they must be refrigerated. Optionally, before storing, lightly douse cake with good brandy, then place a paper towel, folded and doused with brandy over the top, and wrap tightly. Cakes are typically ready 2 weeks after baked and can be stored for 3 months in a cool, dry place, or in fridge. Don't freeze.

The Stoltz family makes these the weekend after Thanksgiving to be given as gifts at Christmas. They are fantastic for desserts, and also make a great snack when hiking, snowshoeing, and skiing throughout the winter.

The Beginning of ENDA December 19, 2013

Recently there was quite an uproar about ENDA— the Employment Non Discrimination Act that gives workplace protection to employees and applicants based on their sexual identity. When I first heard about this, I was surprised; why would we need more legislation for protection of this kind— isn't workplace discrimination already illegal? I was shocked to find out that in some 29 states across the country discrimination is still alive and well. In Louisiana, for e.g. you can still get fired for simply who you are and who you love!

Many "noble" citizens are outraged at this "outrageous bill"; Tony Perkins, a renowned lawmaker, is livid because in his wise words "a law like this wouldn't stop discrimination, it would encourage it against anyone with a traditional view of morality. We all know how the activist community works. Homosexuals and transgenders will use this law to marginalize Christians and take over the market place -- until only their 'lifestyle' is promoted." My question is: who the heck, nominated Perkins as the keeper and protector of Morality and what makes him an expert on "this Homosexual and Transgender community" if he has nothing but hatred toward them? And if I may say so, narrow-minded human beings like Perkins who are unwilling to accept change and are unflinching in their limited views of the world, are the biggest bigots and those that are actually demoralizing morality. These so-called law-abiding lawmakers are worried that many employees would be forced to hire people they would ordinarily choose not to employ and that this law will lead to "frivolous litigation". What I think is that most employees (gay and straight) would themselves refrain from taking up jobs with employers who are creepy to start with instead of making it their life's goal to take up unwelcome jobs with the sole intention of taking their bosses to court.

Don't these privileged lawmakers get it that most average people (yes—gay and straight) are simply trying to make an honest living with the only vested interest of getting by day to day?

I probably sound like a broken record by now but so do many of our supposedly knowledgeable lawmakers who come up with the most preposterous arguments, the sum of which is that Enda is a "bad law". Can someone please explain to me, how **any law** that **prevents discrimination**, can ever be "bad"? And finally, the icing on the ENDA case— this law applies to everyone except the military and religious organizations. Apparently those who serve our country and those who serve God have a mighty divine right to treat their brothers and sisters as less than equal.

The above column is lovingly dedicated to my co-worker Marta Barbosa who makes our workplace fun, creative but above all-- moral!

Karen Feeney's Fruit Delight

1 stick of butter
1 Box of vanilla wafers
1 container of Cool Whip
2 cups of Powdered Sugar
2-16 oz. cans of crushed pineapples (Drained)
2-8 oz. Cream Cheese (softened)
3 Bananas (medium)
2 Quarts Strawberries (Frozen Berries Drained) or Fresh when available (sliced)

Chopped walnuts to cover top

Pan size 13 x 9. Chill & Serve.

In a bowl put crushed vanilla wafers; melt butter and then pour over crushed wafers and mix. Then evenly press wafer mixture into the bottom of pan chill until set (approx. 15 minutes).

Mix together in a bowl:

Cream cheese, Cool Whip, sugar. Spread mixture on top of chilled wafer base. Slice bananas to cover 1 layer. Layer 2 Quarts. of strawberries & pineapples. Top with Cool Whip and sprinkle chopped nuts over Cool Whip topping and fresh strawberries when in season.

Thank you to my friend Karen for sharing the above recipe, which is a true delight just, like her!

December 26, 2013

My son's action the other day made me realize that my unhealthy obsession with baking is rubbing off on my poor kids. When given a mound of modeling clay, he did not make a Stegosaurus or a Giant Earthworm like most 4 year olds but "baked" a cupcake like Mama. Although the candle was big enough to light up my house (and my heart) & the icing a tad bit intense, I was humbly reminded once again that our actions (good and not-so-good) have an indelible effect on our little munchkins. Okay so I promise to be better next time….

Happy New Year friends!

"World's Best" Mac & Cheese
(Adapted & modified from Original Beecher's recipe)

12 ounces penne pasta
Sauce (recipe follows)
1 ounce (1/4 cup) cheddar cheese, grated
1 ounce (1/4 cup) Gruyere cheese, grated
½ teaspoon chipotle chili flakes (optional)
1 cup of Chorizo or Linguica sausage (cut up into small pieces and pan fried)

Cheese Sauce

½ stick unsalted butter
⅓ cup all-purpose flour
3 cups milk
14 ounces Aged Cheddar cheese, grated
2 ounces semi-soft Monterey Jack cheese, grated
4 ounces Grand Cru original cheese
½ teaspoon kosher salt
⅛ teaspoon garlic powder

Melt the butter in a saucepan over medium heat and whisk in the flour. Continue whisking and cook for 2 minutes.

Slowly add the milk, whisking constantly. Cook until the sauce thickens, about 10 minutes, stirring frequently. Remove from the heat.

Add the cheese, salt, chili flakes, and garlic powder. Stir until the cheese is melted and all ingredients are incorporated.

Preheat the oven to 350°F.

Cook the penne 2 minutes less than package directions.

Combine the cooked pasta and Sauce in a medium bowl and mix thoroughly. Scrape the pasta into an 8-inch baking dish. Mix the cooked sausage. Sprinkle the top with the cheese.

Bake, uncovered, for 20/25 minutes. Fantastic!!!

January 2, 2014

My New Year's Resolution this year (and every year from now on) is to make more people cry. After years of making and breaking resolves, I have finally figured out how I can make me happy— make others cry…

It's easy to make someone laugh—a funny joke, a wise comeback, a silly impression, crass humor but when you make others cry—know that you have done well.

There is nothing better than doing something so kind and so special for another human being that it melts the toughest soul. Of course, the act that you initiate has to be completely altruistic; there cannot be an iota of self-interest behind it. Random, unexpected acts of kindness fall under this category. Going the extra mile(s) definitely qualifies. And of course, doing something special for someone who has not always been the nicest to you, always counts.

I swear I am not preaching here; I intend to practice what I claim. I resolve to make people cry so that they can continue to smile long after I am gone J

Happy New Year my friend!

Italian Sausage Bread

1 lb fresh or frozen bread dough
1 lb Italian Sausage
1 onion thinly sliced
½ green pepper diced
12 oz mushroom sliced
½ lb Swiss cheese shredded
½ lb Mozzarella cheese shredded

Sauté separately the peppers, the mushrooms and then the onions. Drain. Remove the sausage from the casings and sauté until cooked. Drain and combine with the veggies and the cheeses.

Roll out the dough into a 10x12" rectangle. Spread on the filling. Roll up tightly jelly roll style. Tuck the ends under. Place seam side down on a lightly greased sheet. Cover and let rise at least 30 minutes. Oil the top of bread.

Bake at 350° for 30 to 40 minutes.

Thanks to Aunt Connie for another great recipe!

Innocence Lost January 9, 2014

A 5-year Fitchburg boy is missing—allegedly killed by his mother and her boyfriend. The Department of Children and Families, whose mission statement is "protecting children from abuse and neglect and strengthening families"—did neither. Although DCF was closely associated with Jeremiah's case, the caseworkers did not bother to question his mysterious disappearance even though the family that they were "helping" was clearly disturbed. And that to me is the biggest tragedy.

A social workers union cited their "large caseloads" as the reason for this incidence and warned that "It is only a matter of time before another tragedy occurs" if this problem is left unaddressed. ***How dare they?*** I have only one word for this ridiculous statement: Preposterous! That's because the very nature of a social worker's job, to me, is sacred. If a doctor or nurse fails to administer life-saving medication to sick patients, because there are too many of them needing these drugs, would it be acceptable? A helpless five-year old at the mercy of his unthinkably abusive caregivers, is just as vulnerable.

This is not to say that all DCF workers are inefficient but in this case even one failure is one too many. As a mom and an educator, I fail to understand how an agency whose sole job is protecting the abused and neglected, failed to perform its duty. It is simply unconscionable and no excuse, however strong, can justify the failure of DCF. Protecting the abused and the helpless is not merely a job but a duty of the highest priority. In the end, a helpless 5-year old is DEAD and while his despicable caregivers probably physically murdered him, it was the irresponsible DCF workers who were responsible for his death. There is no sugarcoating the needless killing of a sweet innocent young life that could not trust the monsters he lived with but probably had faith on those who claimed to protect him. Shameful…

Chicken Hawaiian

Slice 1 large onion and place in the bottom of a large baking pan. Salt & pepper the chicken pieces. Place on top of the onions.

Mix together:
¾ cup chili sauce
½ cup soy sauce
¾ cup brown sugar
6 oz. can frozen orange or orange-pineapple juice (undiluted)
1 can mandarin oranges undrained (optional)
1 can (1 lb 4 oz. pineapple chunks, (undrained)

Pour over the chicken and bake at 325° until well browned. Baste occasionally.

Enjoy over plain rice!

Way to Go Mom January 16, 2014

I just dropped my mom off at the airport. This is the woman who is running purely on will power.

Until five years ago mom was the picture of health with boundless energy that made heads turn; until then I had never seen her sick or even stop to rest. And then out of nowhere, the bastard disease preyed on her body and left it broken. But she fought so hard that even death returned her, and although she had to learn to do everything again, like the simple act of walking, she was not ready to give up quite yet. Even the doctors watched in amazement as she proved their dire predictions wrong. She was not meant to make it; yet here she is taking a flight, the first leg of which is seventeen hours long— all by herself. And when I expressed my concern and complained about the long journey that lay ahead (because I know how much the body hurts), she turned to me and said: "Never fret at what might go wrong, look at all the things that have gone right." And when my eyes welled up as we said goodbye, she scolded me and said in her unshakably brave voice: "Don't be sad; think about all the positives and always be happy!" Not a drop of tear shed from the eyes, not a smile ever wiped from the face even though I could clearly detect the stabbing pain of separation and the fear if this might be the last goodbye.

Her enthusiasm kills me but that's what keeps her alive!

My Mom's Pudding

This easy to make pudding was a must-have in all of my festive childhood gatherings. If you like Flan, you will love this dish.

3 cups of milk, cold
3 eggs

1 slice of bread (soaked in milk and then mashed)
Sugar 5 Tbsp.
Vanilla essence 2 Tbsp.

Break eggs in cold milk. Stir to mix well.

Add sugar, soaked bread and vanilla.

In aluminum pudding dish, put 1 Tsp. of sugar. Put over flame till it caramelizes (turns burnt red).

Or, in a Pyrex dish add sugar and put under broiler until the sugar starts to caramelize. Put the milk mixture in and place on a hot water bath (add about 2 cups of water on baking pan/sheet. Bake in oven for about 45 minutes at 350° or until just set but not hard.

Serve it chilled with a chocolate ganache sauce, caramel sauce, whipped cream or garnish with fresh berries. My mom often topped it with raisins and slivered almonds— so good!

Shining Star January 23, 2014

A father and his daughter went outside on Christmas Eve to watch the stars. Soon a squabble about the position of the Big Dipper resulted in the 22-year old stabbing her dad in the chest. I do not know what actually transpired under the open sky but this much I do know-this act of senseless violence was not newsworthy. The T.V. channels made light of this situation, mentioning it casually as one of the "major" news stories-- one more vicious than the next. This to me is a problem bigger than the violence itself. We have grown so accustomed to hearing about violence that we, as a society, have become numb toward these extraordinarily fierce incidents. We begin to accept them as normal, ordinary, everyday happenings when there is nothing ordinary about them. While watching the killings, the stabbings, the abductions, the drunk-driving and the corruptions on Christmas day, I began to wonder why Nurse Ellen who had taken time off her busy schedule to stitch and deliver pillow- cases to the sick children at a local hospital, did not make the 5 o'clock news. There are innumerable Christmas miracles such as these that do not make the headlines. There are amazing acts of grace that I witness around me everyday that do not make the news. The world that we live in is kind but the everyday beautiful people that make this world livable are not sensational enough.

That Christmas night I wondered if all of us are responsible to some degree for yet another falling star.

Marita's Chinese Salad

1 head cabbage
½ bunch of scallions or green onions, chopped
2 Packages of Ramen Noodles; uncooked & broken into pieces (discard seasonings)

2 Tbsp. sunflower seeds
1 cup sliced almonds
¼ cup margarine
½ cup sugar
¼ cup oil
¼ cup red wine vinegar
1 Tbsp. soy sauce

Chop cabbage into medium pieces. Add chopped green onions.

Brown noodles, sunflower seeds, almonds in margarine and set aside to cool.

Boil sugar, vinegar and sugar and cool completely. Toss everything together just before serving.

Doesn't keep well overnight but everything can be made ahead and assembled in the last minute.

The Pope of Good Hope January 30, 2014

According to CNN polls, Pope Francis has an approval rating of 88% -- the highest any other Pope has ever had. As for the remaining 12% -- they would like the Holy Father to judge more.

And as for me, I am thrilled--finally there is a gem at the helm who gets it. Pope Francis is the living embodiment of what we imagine a Supreme Being to be—simple, modest, merciful and humble. If there is a God, Pope Francis represents Him beautifully.

The Papacy since Medieval times has been anything but simple; pomp & splendor have been its cornerstone. Its leaders have always been elitist and thus, beyond the reach of its ordinary followers, even though its Messiah was as ordinary as it gets. The Pope has gloriously descended from the golden pedestal upon which he was placed for over two thousand years and has shed his "holier than thou" attitude along with the extravagant trappings that come with the office. "The worst thing that could happen to the Church", he has said on many occasions, "is what de Lubac called spiritual worldliness".

It is refreshing to see the Pope treating humans as humans and not merely as objects of proselytization. The Pope is genuinely kind to everyone-- the sick, the needy, the disfigured, the ordinary, the four-legged, the complicated, the criminal, the faithful, but most importantly, the **non-believer**. This, to me, is of utmost importance. We all can learn to get along with those with whom we feel a certain kinship, who are in some ways, like us, and who share something common with us whether it is race, ethnicity, religion, faith or culture but the true test of a saint (or an ordinary saintly person) is when he looks at another being and sees simply that—another precious being. A simple concept but one that is infinitely difficult to practice!

Marx claimed that "Religion is the opium of the masses" and after closely following the Holy Father, I feel that Religion such as **his** is a necessary opiate to be experienced & enjoyed by all.

Cetta's Basic Pesto

3 cups loosely packed fresh basil leaves
⅓ cup Pine nuts (Pignola)
3 garlic cloves
½ cup olive oil
Salt & freshly ground black pepper to taste

Place basil, pine nuts and garlic in a food processor and mix until everything is well chopped.

Slowly add oil in a thin stream to form a fairly smooth paste.

Pesto will keep refrigerated for a couple of weeks. Keep in an airtight container and cover with a thin layer of olive oil to prevent discoloring.

Pesto freezes well.

Use a spoonful or two for a bowl of perfect pasta. Sprinkle Parmesan cheese on top.

An Olympic Salute February 7, 2014

In his 5th year in office, President Obama is catching a lot of flack. From the Obamacare fiasco to the state of economy, from the withdrawal of troops in Iraq to a flip-flop with Syria-- the President has collected enough scorn to almost rival his predecessor George W. However, in an amazing feat of fairness and wisdom, he completely won me over again.

Mr. Obama deserves a gold medal for assembling a glorious team to represent "US" in the Olympic games. Sending openly gay athletes to Russia is a statement to the world that the United States of America is much more than a country of oil thirsty warmongers or profit hungry capitalists or even geographically challenged patriotic zealots-- as is widely believed. America *is* Freedom-- not just freedom from oppressive Governments and groups, but also freedom from bias and double standards.

Thank you Mr. President for validating once more that our vote in the last two elections has bought us a little piece of American Style Freedom. And Thank you also for keeping the Olympic spirit alive!

"The most important thing in the Olympic Games is not to win but to take part, just as the most important thing in life is not the triumph but the struggle. The essential thing is not to have conquered but to have fought well." -- the Olympic Creed

All American Banana Bread

½ cup Crisco (shortening, can substitute butter)
1 ½ cups sugar
2 eggs
1 cup crushed bananas

1 tsp. vanilla
2 cups flour
1 tsp. baking soda
½ tsp. cinnamon
½ cup buttermilk

Cream shortening and sugar. Add eggs, banana, and vanilla. In a different bowl, sift dry ingredients together and add to the creamed mixture. Add buttermilk, beat until smooth. Pour in loaf pan. Bake at 350° for 1 hour. (I can't remember who took the time to share this hand-written recipe with me but I want to say **Thank You** for the best Banana Bread ever)!

This one is for you... February 13, 2014

I am so grateful for you my friend!

Nearly 20 years ago when I first arrived in Boston, I knew exactly one person here—my nicer half. And now, I am starting to choke up as I write about the relationships and friendships that I have formed with my friends—too many to mention. Many of these friendships started in the most unlikely of places and with people who, on the outside, are nothing like me. But as I have gotten to know you, I have realized that what we see is truly not half as important as what we cannot see. Yes, the roots within a family run deep (and often you can't severe those ties even if they are strangling you) but what I have realized is that just as deep run the bonds that connect me with those who were once complete strangers— who spoke a language that was different from mine, who grew up in a planet that was alien to me, and who most certainly prayed to a different God than I did (but I guess our Gods were kind & showered us with the gift of friendship and that makes me wonder if our Gods were really that different but I digress...).

I had always believed that one true friend is better than many acquaintances but I am truly blessed to have many, many true friends—each one more special than the next. Some of you I have met through work, some through play, some in the most unlikeliest of places: yet now I can unequivocally say that my life would not be complete without you, even if we share just a "Hi" at work, a "Hello" on the phone, an occasional **"smile"** via text, have a casual visit or if lucky, a planned get-together. You are the kind of friend that makes me smile when I think about you. So here's to you my dear, dear friend- you are who touches me deep inside yet for you I have no words but only a heartfelt "Thank You". And lucky for me, I came across this quote from Thoreau, who too was well versed on this most beautiful relationship: *"The language of friendship is not words but meanings"*.

The above column is dedicated to my loving friend **Jina Guimond** and all of you who make life lovely. Happy Valentines Day, friends!

Love,
Rumni

Here's a simple yet absolutely fabulous dish for your loved ones, slightly modified but borrowed from the Pioneer Woman. (May I also mention that Jina loved it?)

Shrimp Penne

12 ounces penne pasta
8 ounces large shrimp
2 tablespoons butter
2 tablespoons olive oil
2 cloves garlic, finely chopped
1 small onion, finely chopped
1/2 cup white wine, optional (I use chicken stock)
1- 14.5-ounce can tomato sauce
1-cup heavy cream
1/4 cup chopped parsley
6 leaves fresh basil, cut in chiffonade
Freshly ground black pepper
Crusty French bread, for serving

Directions

Bring a pot of lightly salted water to a boil. Cook the penne until al dente. Drain and set aside.

Begin by peeling and deveining the shrimp and rinsing them under cold water. Remove the tails from the shrimp, chop into medium-size pieces.

In a large skillet over medium-high heat, add 1 tablespoon of the butter and 1 tablespoon of the olive oil. When the pan is hot, add the shrimp. Stir and cook on both sides until just starting to turn opaque, about 2 minutes. Remove to a plate and allow to cool slightly.

In a large skillet over medium heat, add the remaining 1 tbsp. butter and 1 tbsp. olive oil. Add the garlic and onion. Stir to combine and cook, stirring occasionally, until the onion is translucent, about 3 minutes.

Pour the wine into the pan if using. Stir and allow it to evaporate, about 45 seconds. Pour in the tomato sauce and stir to combine. Reduce the heat to low. Pour in the cream. Stir well to combine; reduce the heat to simmer.

Add the shrimp to the sauce and stir gently to combine.

Next, add in the parsley and basil and stir. Add the cooked, drained pasta. Stir gently to coat. Add salt and freshly ground black pepper. Be sure to taste the seasonings at the end, adjusting if necessary.

Serve with more wine.

What were they thinking? February 20, 2014

How is it that the interpreter at Mr. Mandela's funeral was an imposter who signed 100% incorrectly? Thamsanqa Jantjie claimed to be seeing angels the whole time he was up on stage but continued to make gestures— all ridiculously phony. How does a mentally unstable, ex-convict get hired to do one of the most important jobs under the watchful eyes of the world? And where does this kind of audacity come from?

How is it that the healthcare.gov website went down as soon as it went up? This is of course after years in planning and millions in expenditure. If my 5 year old asks me to do something (reasonable- of course), I make sure it gets done; can't imagine what would happen if the President of the United States gives me a directive and agrees to pay me over $500 million for the job. Apparently the Montreal-based CGI group responsible for the website was replaced by the Dublin-based Accenture Group after it failed to deliver to the President. My question is: what the heck were the 400+ CGI employees, working around the clock for over 3 months, working on?

How in the world was the most important word on the commemorative coin to mark Pope Francis' election to the Papacy spelled wrong? How does "Jesus" become "Lesus" and no one notices until long after these precious coins start circulating in the market? What in God's name was the Vatican musing when minting this momentous memento? I wonder…

Here's a simple recipe shared to me by Lynn Piana, a wonderful secretary at GMS:

Bacon and Egg Casserole

7-8 large eggs
1-½ cups milk
1 large loaf of Italian bread
1 bag shredded cheddar cheese
1 lb. bacon
Salt and pepper to taste

Break Italian bread into small pieces in a 9x13 casserole dish. Cook bacon and break into pieces on top of bread. Sprinkle cheddar cheese. Mix eggs and milk together, pour evenly over other ingredients. Bake at 350° for 45 minutes.

Lynn's expert Note: "I usually cover with tin foil and take off for last 10 minutes".

Enjoy!

Trapped Feb 27, 2014

The Massachusetts Appeals Court recently ruled that Michelle Kosilek, a convicted murderer and transgender person currently serving a life sentence without parole—will undergo a tax-funded sex change operation. This is on top of the $700,000 in legal bills that he racked up in his defense for brutally murdering his wife that we must now clear. On May 20, 1990 Michelle (then Robert) used a bail wire to strangulate and nearly decapitate his wife Cheryl—a Substance Abuse Counselor, whom he had met while undergoing alcohol & drug treatment and who tried to give him a stable home after what he claims to be years of oppression by the world.

I do understand that Gender Identity Dysphoria (GID) is a real disorder and I also believe that Michelle is probably undergoing psychological trauma trapped in what he claims to be a "man's body". But at the same time I am having a hard time sympathizing with a cold-blooded killer especially when I know that there are many law-abiding, decent individuals who are suffering from GID but are unable to undergo a sex change operation because of lack of resources (or is it because they have not committed a gruesome crime?)

The Massachusetts Court says that it is only right that we provide Gender Reassignment Service to Mr. Kosilek. Really? Well, how about providing a Death Reassignment Service to Mrs. Kosilek?

Justice is supposed to be blind not bovine.

Vegetarian Chili

1-Tbsp. oil
1 medium onion, chopped

1-Tbsp. ground cumin
1-Tbsp. dried oregano
Salt & pepper to taste
2 bell peppers, chopped
3 cloves garlic, chopped
1 Tbsp. chipotle in adobo sauce (freeze the rest in a zip lock bag for use as needed)
1-28 ounce can crushed tomatoes
2 Tspn. chili powder
2 Tbspn. sugar to balance the tomatoes
1 can of broth or a cup of water
1 (15 ounce) can kidney beans, drained
1 (15 ounce) can garbanzo beans, drained
1 (15 ounce) can black beans
1 small bag of frozen sweet corn.

Heat the oil in a large pot over medium heat. Stir in the onions and peppers, and season with cumin, oregano, and sugar. Cook and stir on low until onion is tender, then mix in the garlic, and chipotle pepper. Let cook for a minute or two stirring frequently. Mix the tomatoes into the pot. Season with chili powder, salt & pepper. Add the broth/water. Stir in the drained kidney beans, garbanzo beans, and black beans. Bring to a boil, reduce heat to low, and simmer about 45 minutes. Stir in the corn, and continue cooking 5 minutes before serving. Serve with toppings of your choice: cheese, cilantro, sour cream, red onions! Freezes very well!

Crazy Busy March 6, 2014

It was a blustery thirteen degrees at 7 P.M. As I was running around trying to get dinner on the table, my husband called asking me to pull out of the driveway so he could get in. As I grabbed the keys and dashed out of the door, my phone rang again. It was my son asking me to pick him up from wrestling practice "now". As I rushed out again, cursing to myself about how no one gives me a moment of peace, my eyes caught a glimpse of the neighbor's house- pitch dark except for a dim porch light that is always left on.

About thirteen years ago when we first moved to our house, the McMullen's front light flickered on and off all evening long in response to the constant stream of people in & out of the door. The 5 kids and their never-ending activities ensured that the front door was always open and mom or dad was chaperoning one, some or all of the kids at all times. As I looked closer I noticed that the snow from the car had not been brushed off which meant that Mrs. McMullen had not left the house for at least 4 days when the last snow had fallen-- (the kids have all moved out since and Mr. McMullen no longer drives because of his fading health). As I looked once more at the black car with the thick white top and the thicker white windshield, I realized how incredibly lucky I am to have my crazy life. How fortunate I am to be needed "now"! How wonderful this crazy busy life is and how much I love the liveliness that lights up my driveway (and warms my heart)! In that busy shuffle I promised myself that I will never forget the cold snow atop the McMullen's car and the stillness inside their big brown house.

The Best Tomato Soup Ever

2 large cans of whole tomatoes
4 cloves garlic- chopped

2 cups chicken broth
1-Tsp. butter
4-Tbsp. sugar
½ cup cream
Salt & pepper to taste
Fresh Basil

Drain tomatoes in sieve over a pot. Reserve the liquid.

On a baking sheet lined with foil, roast the drained tomatoes in a 450° oven for about 30 minutes. Make sure to turn halfway (you can also broil them toward the end if they are not getting charred or if you run out of patience like me).

Add the roasted tomatoes to the reserved liquid and blend well in a blender.

In a large pot, heat the butter; add garlic and sauté for a few minutes making sure not to burn.

Put the liquid back into the pot, add the broth and cook for about 20 minutes. Add the cream and simmer away until thickened. Add sugar, salt & pepper and check for seasoning. (The soup tastes best on the sweeter side but feel free to eliminate the sugar if you are watching your diet).

Serve with basil chiffonade and an accompanying grilled cheese sandwich. Be on the lookout for a deliciously easy, gourmet grilled cheese recipe in next week's paper.

Checked Out March 13, 2014

I was at the checkout counter of my local Wal-Mart with a month's worth of staples in my cart. A woman with the biggest scowl (& camouflage pajamas) stood behind me complaining to her companion. I was in a great mood and nothing was going to bring me down- not even an ugly attitude. Her guy companion took charge and moved to another lane. Within minutes, the two returned, clearly having lost what they thought was their place to someone else. This time they were armed with bigger attitudes and nastier scowls. The woman turned to her man and yelled: "You are an idiot; you don't use your head- that's the problem. Just look at her"-- pointing toward my overflowing cart, completely unaware or uncaring that others (and I) may be looking on. She went on & on about how he was so stupid and that she was not going to "come over tonight". (What a blessing- I thought!) The man stood there barely muttering a word or two like "Why?" and "What did I do?" to which she yelled profanities even more. This interaction was most painful to watch and frankly, quite embarrassing but the "lady" was oblivious of her surroundings.

When it was my turn to pay, I struck up a conversation with the cashier just so I could drown out the nasty exchanges between the very loving couple. No sooner than I began speaking that the man turned to me and said in a most unpleasant tone: "Hey- it is a very busy time; why don't you just let the man work?" My initial reaction was to say something even nastier to him like: "Why don't *you* stand up to your lady friend instead of telling me what to do?" but restrained myself. I turned nervously to the cashier but gathered up enough strength to ask: "Am I bothering you?" to which he answered sheepishly, "Of course not; I enjoy talking to people. It is always chaos here but I realize it takes all kinds of people". With a genuine smile and a sly wink, the nice gentleman continued to chat pleasantly while the two behind me continued to deride each other ruthlessly. Indeed, it takes all kinds of people…

A heart-felt "Thank you" to the easy-going and hard-working folks like ***Mark Geisser*** *whose generous smile makes the sometimes-unfriendly world bearable.*

Grilled Cheese Sandwich with a Twist

For each sandwich you will need:
1-2 slices of mozzarella cheese
1-2 slices of sharp cheddar cheese
2 thick slices of multi-grain bread
4-5 pieces of chopped scallion (a must try)
Butter

Assemble sandwich by layering the two kinds of cheese and then adding scallion pieces. In a buttered pan, cook the sandwich until cheese melts- about 3 minutes per side. (Tip: You may use a griddle or an electric grill for making a big batch at once; also feel free to experiment with different kinds of meat, ham or even bacon to add another layer of yummy goodness). Cut in half and watch the molten cheese ooze out!

Presidential Duty March 20, 2014

Dr. Gwendolyn Boyd was recently elected President of Alabama Sate University. This is a momentous election— that of the first woman President in the instituition's181 year-old history. This is a big step towards equality between the sexes— right? Wrong! Apparently, there is a stipulation in Dr. Boyd's contract which states that "for so long as Dr. Boyd is President and a single person, she shall not be allowed to cohabitate in the President's residence with any person with whom she has a romantic relation." The University claims that the Office of the President has a moral responsibility to represent the school she leads. I get that; however I don't understand why such a condition was made part of the legal jargon. One would think that the trustees have enough faith in the person they hired to make the right judgment after a rigorous search. (To give you an idea of how intense the process was, a private investigator was hired through the committee's law firm, Maynard, Cooper & Gale, to conduct extensive background screenings of the candidates.)

If Dr. Boyd fit the mold and is good enough to make appropriate decisions in her professional life, why can't she be trusted to do the same in her personal life? Why does there need to be an insurance policy to ensure "right-doing"?

I don't get the logic- does the Board of Trustees believe that such a provision would ward off potential co-habitation among the student body? Yeah-right! And even if so, what then? I am very confused! This is akin to Marty Walsh being ousted from his duly elected position as the Mayor of Boston for sharing a home with the "love of his life" and long time partner Mary Higgins. Laughable- this is; equality- this is not.

Sloppy Joes (Modified from Ree Drummond's Original recipe)

2-pounds ground beef
1 large green bell pepper, diced
½ large onion, diced
1- cup ketchup
5 cloves garlic, minced
2 Tbsp. packed brown sugar
1 Tsp. chili powder
1 Tsp. dry mustard
1-Tbsp.Worcestershire sauce
Salt and pepper
8 kaiser rolls
2- Tbsp. butter

Start by browning the ground beef. Set aside. Drain most of the fat.

In the remaining fat, add the onions and then peppers. Add the garlic & and sauté. Add the ketchup, brown sugar, chili powder, dry mustard, Worcestershire, salt and pepper to taste. Add a cup of water, stir to combine, and then cover and simmer over medium-low heat, about 20 minutes.

To serve, spread the rolls with the butter and brown them on a skillet. Spoon a generous amount of the meat mixture onto the bottom roll, and then top with the other half. Serve with chips or if feeling too guilty- choose carrot sticks instead.

Try this recipe and I promise you will never look at the red can again. I don't know if that's a good thing....

Death Watch March 27, 2014

The other day I heard about the ultimate gadget- a wristwatch that claims to count down your life. I was quite shocked to find out that this is just one of many such products on the market that serves the same morbid purpose i.e., count down the days until you die. Answer a few essential questions and the watch comes up with the date of your impending death. The entrepreneurs pushing these bizarre products claim that having such a device close at hand will make you and me a better person. I do not think so…

I do not need anyone or anything telling me that I am not invincible or indispensable. I just want to travel the road happy while denying that I will ever run out of time. If and when the clock does stop ticking, I promise to go along but for now I'd rather go along with Woody Allen who spoke my mind about this utterly unnecessary reality:

"I'm not afraid of death; I just don't want to be there when it happens."

Best & Easiest Cookies

2¼ cups flour
1-Tsp. baking soda
1-Tsp. baking powder
½ Tsp. salt
1-cup butter, softened
¾- cup brown sugar, packed
¼- cup granulated sugar
1-(3.4 oz.) box instant pudding (white chocolate flavored)
2 eggs
1-Tbsp. vanilla extract
2-cups semi white chocolate chips
1-cup dried cranberries

1. Preheat oven to 350° and line cookie sheets with parchment paper.
2. In a large bowl sift flour, baking soda, baking powder and salt together. Set aside.
3. Beat butter, brown sugar, granulated sugar and pudding mix well.
4. Add eggs.
5. Add vanilla extract.
6. Slowly add flour mixture and mix until combined.
7. Add chips and cranberries and mix.
8. Place a generous heaping Tbsp. of dough on cookie sheets and bake for 10-12 minutes. Enjoy!

Thank you to Miss Jhoselin for sharing this amazing cookie recipe with me!

Feel free to add your favorite bits like butterscotch and almond bark- endless possibilities to call them your own!

Ordinary Heroes April 3, 2014

I would like to dedicate today's column to the ordinary folks who come to work every day and put up the bravest front in spite of being broken inside. There is something remarkably amazing in what they so deliberately yet effortlessly do.

Life, as we all know, is not always kind to us. Sometimes things happen that are, at best, utterly unfair.

I was in high school when I lost my dad; my life came to a long halt following this untimely jolt. I was devastated; I did not smile for almost a year— at home or at school. You may argue that I was only seventeen then but it wasn't my tender age—it is my nature.

There was a time five years ago when my mother was very sick -- to the point that her doctors had written her off. I did come to work every day but I was not myself- inside or out. I was barely present and did not want to engage in any conversation with anyone, even though I couldn't have asked for nicer colleagues and greater support. At home, I was no better. My family saw a sad image of my former self as I constantly wallowed in self-pity. Yes - I was being selfish once again, and that's precisely why when I see the remarkable, consummate professionals around me who are battling personal tragedies -- be it their own serious illness, the illness or even death of a loved one -- I have nothing but the utmost respect. How courageous of them to have the ability to separate themselves from a life-altering situation and give it their best to everyone around them! How admirable of them to contain their indescribable sorrow! How brave of them to put on a happy face so as to make others comfortable even when the wound is raw and is slowly but surely eating away at their soul. Ordinary, everyday life but extraordinary heroism!

"Let me not pray to be sheltered from dangers but to be fearless in facing them. Let me not beg for the stilling of my pain, but for the heart to conquer it."—***Rabindranath Tagore***

Spinach Pesto Tacos

Pound of chicken/turkey (ground)
1 package of taco seasoning
Box of frozen spinach (thawed & drained)
1 cup of pesto
Salsa (bought from produce section- drained slightly so it is not so watery)
2 cups of Monterey Jack cheese
Hard taco shells

Cook the chicken; add taco seasoning, spinach, pesto & salsa. Let combine.

In a baking dish line up taco shells and stand them all up. Stuff, cover with cheese & bake at 425° for 10 minutes.

Thank you Miss Alicia for this wonderful recipe!

Teenage Boys April 10, 2014

Why is it that they never turn off the lights while leaving their own rooms but turn off the kitchen lights when *I* am still in there cooking?

Why is it that they complain that *you* are too loud when the music they are listening to is blasting through the roofs?

Why is it that they walk through the front door complaining that the house smells nasty when their own room is a perpetual pigsty?

Why is it that they are so reluctant to take a shower yet douse themselves with body spray?

Why is it that they give you a hard time at every meal when they are perfectly happy to devour Oatmeal at a friend's house?

Why is it that they are so rude to their own parents when everyone else's parents think of them as the most polite things alive?

But the most distressing of them all— why do these obnoxious, clueless yet utterly loveable creatures grow up *so* darned fast?

Broccoli & Cheese Dip

A box of chopped or broccoli cuts (frozen)- thawed & drained

16 oz. container of sour cream

1 package of dry vegetable soup mix

1 cup of shredded cheddar cheese

Mix everything in a square Pyrex dish and bake in a 350° oven for 20/30 minutes until bubbly. Serve with Pita chips.

A big Thank you to Jane Coppinger for well stocking my Dip Recipes!

April 17, 2014

My little guy turns 6 today. Here's a sampling of the stimulating conversations we've had over the years.

Tell me more…

Mom, you are like an elephant when you run. You stomp and make the dirt fly. That is so cool mom!

(Am I supposed to feel happy?)

Faint- it's like you die but you wake up from your dying.

Mom, are the Kratt Brothers real? (The Wild Kratts is an animated PBS show based on the real-life animal conservationists Chris and Martin Kratt).

Mom: *Yes!*

Really?

Mom: *Yess*

But are they soft like Disneyland or are they hard like us?

("Hard"- now that explains us alright).

Mom, my snortils are itchy.

(I think he means nostrils).

Can you please ask the internet mom?

Finally understanding how to change the pillowcase after struggling with the process:

Oh, I get it- I have to make it into a chicken nugget!

Mom: *What?*

The pillow is the chicken and the case is like the crust.

(I have never looked at a pillow the same way since.)

Mom, do you know what Hulap lizards are?

Mom: Never heard of them.

They are lizards that have a little thing that hangs around their neck.

Mom: *Really—that's interesting because I swear I thought they were called Dewlap Lizards."*

(Confidently) No, silly mommy! It's called Hulap because the lizard can swing it like a hula hoop.

(Come to think of it- Hulap does make more sense).

Mom, is it called "cancel" because u have to cancel all your plans?

(Upon finding out that "cancer/l" is a serious illness).

Mom, bro was on his phone, showing his furry legs to a friend while you were gone. But don't worry- I took care of it; I told her: Get outta here!!!

(It's wonderful having an innocent-looking spy watching over a teenager!)

Mom, I'm sad; Logan does not like me.

Mom: *There will always be some people who will like you & some who won't.*

And some who ***you*** *will really like but who won't like you back. I am sad again Mommy!*

While trying to explain to me something that happened the day before, the poor kid kept struggling with the concept of time. Finally, the gleam in his eyes alerted me that he got it!

Mom: *So, when did this happen again?*

Tomorrow-- pointing the other way.

The best thing happened to Ms. O. today.

Mom: *Really? What?*

She is a grandmother!

Mom: *That's awesome! Is it her son or her daughter who had the baby?*

It must be her daughter because men can't lay babies-- you know.

Mom: *Goodbye, love- I have to leave now.*

Ok- Sionardo, mom.

(I love my little linguist)!

Happy Birthday baby! Keep smiling and make others smile- always…

R2's Favorite Chocolate Mousse

1 (3.9 ounce) package instant chocolate pudding mix

1½ cups milk
1 (16 ounce) container thawed, whipped topping

Prepare the pudding in a large bowl using 1½ cups of milk.

Fold in the whipped topping until blended. Refrigerate until chilled and serve. A delectable treat for the loves in your life!

WICKED AWESOME April 24, 2014

Today I saw a sea of humanity that made me PROUD to be a human again. There were countless faces, each unique and each with a uniquely different story but they all had one thing in common- a pride that transcended everything else. The physical pain that the body experienced was overcome by the pride that the heart felt to be part of "Boston Strong". The sense of kinship and allegiance to a city that was bruised, and needed to be healed- through utter defiance- was utterly contagious. The smiles and cheers screamed out loud that this is a city like no other, a city whose people refuse to bow down to tragedy and cower down in the face of evil. This is a city whose heart beats as one; a city that hurts and heals as one-- a city that rises above that crippling pain to win the race- together. For those 26.2 miles, it did not matter whether you were young or old, black, white or brown, whether you worshipped Jeremiah or Jesus, whether you believed in anything or nothing-- on that sacred course your spirit dared not be touched.

As I stood there- my eyes welling up and my voice starting to choke, I was prouder than ever to be just an ordinary person cheering for another. I could feel the blood pumping through every heart; in that moment we were not complete strangers separated by metal barricades but joined together with a common thread- to heal a city that was hurting.

As the last wave passed and the screams got even louder, I realized that the proud Bostonians had regained what was rightfully theirs- with style, grace and tenacity. Humanity that had been tainted a year ago had become victorious again. Today Boston scored a collective victory like never before. Today I am more proud than ever to say that "Boston you are my home".

Mrs. Coppinger's Hot Pepperoni Layered Dip

In a square Pyrex dish add the following:

Block of cream cheese (8 oz.)— spread on the bottom of the dish.

Pour a small jar of pizza sauce.

Chopped onions (½ cup)

Add ½ package of pepperoni (quartered)

Shredded Italian cheese (1 cup)

Remaining package of pepperoni

Bake at 350° for 20/30 minutes. Serve with a long loaf of French bread.

Restoring Hope May 1, 2014

A 75-year old woman was recently found in a 9 x 6 basement room under deplorable conditions. The fire fighters who responded to this heartrending scene on a bitter cold February day, reported that the heat was turned off and the woman was confined to a hospital bed -- starved, dehydrated and her body covered with open bedsores. In spite of the severity of the abuse she had invariably endured, she was conscious of her situation, which makes this story even more tragic. How long, I wonder, did this poor soul suffer the most horrific torture and a sense of utter hopelessness? Just to give you an idea-- this unimaginable condition did not develop overnight; bed sores so severe that they eat away the skin to the point of exposing the bones, are formed when patients are bedridden for prolonged periods of time without changing position. Even the first responders who found her were clearly shaken and described this as "one of the worst cases of elder abuse they have ever seen". A registered nurse and caretaker has been charged with this severe abuse.

I do not know how this case will play out in the courts; all I know is that I do not wish such misfortune upon anyone- no matter who she is or what she was ever like. I have been plagued by a million questions since the first time I saw this tragedy unfold. Perhaps you can help me. How does a person, in a civilized society, get to a point in her life where something so horrific such as this can occur away from the watchful eyes of her loved ones? Are some amongst us so unfortunate that no one cares if we are alive or dead or even barely living? What happened to the relationships that were formed along the way that allowed such an atrocity to be committed? How is it that a living, breathing human being is left to fester away in a basement without food or water for days on end? What happened to basic human dignity and compassion? How can we as a society allow even one such woefully shameful incident to occur? Unfortunately a case such as this is more common than we would like to believe. According to the Administration on Aging, "Each year hundreds of thousands of elders are abused, neglected, and exploited and for every reported incident of elder abuse, five others go unreported". This means that as I write this piece in utter disbelief, there are many monsters like Sandra Calixte Lucien preying on many more helpless victims like Marie Bois Belfort. Revolting but true!

This article is devoted to tortured souls like Marie who are suffering needlessly in the hands of the heartless, disguised as caregivers. Even though the situation seems utterly helpless, I do believe that every problem has a solution and we can all do our part, however small, to make a big difference in the life of another. As such, I am requesting us to make a concerted effort to check on our elderly neighbors from time to time and to also visit the Department of Health and Human Services website: http://www.aoa.gov/AoA_programs/Elder_Rights/EA_Prevention/whatIsEA.aspx. Let's do whatever we can to save the life and dignity of a helpless elder who could well be a loved one (or even you or me) under the most unfortunate of circumstances someday. Think about it….

MARY'S APPLE CRISP

- Preheat oven at 350°.
- Slice about 6 big Apples (thin).
- Pour into greased pie dish or pan.
- Pour in ½ cup of water.
- Sprinkle Cinnamon on top.

Mix:

1 cup of flour

1 cup of sugar

1 stick of soft butter (do not melt)

Mix with hands until crumbly.

Sprinkle mixture on top of apples.

Bake for 1 Hour.

Tough Love May 8, 2014

Today I have something simple to share- it's just that I feel genuinely happy for a friend.

You know- I love writing. I also love getting feedback about my writing. The other day a friend of mine told me after reading the January 16 article about my mom that she "liked it". Simple words but genuine coming from someone who I know has had a very tough mother/daughter relationship. I thanked her with a smile and knowing the situation, said nothing but felt something.

The next week my friend came to me with all her strength trying to fight back the tears from her big brown eyes. She told me that my column had got her thinking and she had come to the realization that she could not live with herself if something happened to her mom. So she had made contact with her mother— talked about simple, mundane things. I could see how difficult this must have been and how this seemingly simple act must have been a giant step, years in the making for this is about tending the most precious relationship and healing an old wound that hurts more with time.

Good for her-- for how many of us go through life never finding the strength until it is too late?

And good luck my friend rediscovering repressed love!

"If someone you love hurts you-- cry a river, build a bridge, and get over it."--Anonymous

Happy Mother's Day friends!

My Friend Sudarshana's Easy Seafood Linguine

olive oil-3 Tbs.
butter-2 Tbsp.
fresh garlic 2- 3 cloves, chopped
fresh parsley chopped (1/4 cup + 2tbsp)
½ Tsp. red pepper flakes (optional)
seafood of choice
½ cup of very dry white wine (Sudarshana says "My favorite is Beach house- it has a screw cap, but I still love it. Remember to put the remaining wine- if you don't drink it all while cooking, in the fridge until dinnertime")
Salt to taste
bread crumbs- 1/2 cup
grated Parmesan
wedges of lemon
1 package pasta (preferably linguine)

Heat 2 Tbsp. olive oil and butter in pan, add garlic, ¼ cup parsley, stir quickly till aromatic on medium heat. Add seafood- in order of firmness, mussels go first, stir to coat evenly, add 1 cup water, bring to boil, cover and simmer until all mussels are open- discard any that don't open. Cook down water if necessary, add shrimp, squid and scallops in that order if using, stir and add wine; allow to cook down a bit on high heat; add red pepper flakes and salt to taste. Turn off heat.

Boil pasta to slightly firmer than al dente, retain ½ cup of pasta water, drain and add pasta to seafood mixture, toss well for a min, turn on heat again, add the pasta water, allowing it to thicken the liquid in the pot a little bit; quickly remove from heat and put in individual serving bowls.

Heat 1 Tbsp. of evoo to smoking in a pan, add breadcrumbs and remaining 2 tbsp chopped parsley; toss quickly. Sprinkle this mixture over the pasta along with a little (very little) bit of parm. Stick a wedge of lemon in every bowl, and serve with a green salad, a quality good crusty bread and the wine you put in the fridge earlier. Enjoy!

Note: Scallops are notoriously easy to overcook- you might find it easier to sear them separately and add them to the mixture at the last minute with the pasta water

EX-terminator May 15, 2014

Recently I met the world's most eager salesman. "Joe Jr.", as he insisted on being called, made a house call for a free quote to eliminate our pesky pests that make their rounds every spring. Joe Jr. was professional, courteous and oozing with enthusiasm while discussing "the best pest management and protection plan tailored to each family's needs". (I did not realize that there was more than one way to eradicate ants but apparently there is, depending on the "Platinum, Gold or Silver Plan that one chooses". It goes without saying that the more money you spend, the more bugs you kill, and of course keep killed longer).

Joe Jr. asked only about a few hundred times if I had any questions after explaining everything about several hundred times. (He also insisted on leaving me his cell number "just in case you think of something afterwards"). It was 6 P.M. on a Tuesday evening and all I was thinking was when he would be done talking, when we would be able to devour dinner, how- at this unearthly hour- did he still have the energy to talk about ants, mice and termites and how (for pure application purposes) was his shirt impeccably white after hours of inspecting numerous basements, attics and foundations? It did not deter him in the slightest when I suddenly terminated our conversation and after severing all eye contact, started furiously concocting the most pungent Fish Sauce in the kitchen. I swear I would have signed up for the Ultra Platinum Plus Plan that very moment even if I had to take out a second mortgage just to make Joe Jr. stop talking but he insisted that I not rush, discuss this over with my family (like they cared!) and calmly make a decision after looking over the material that he was leaving behind for me.

It has been a week since I met Joe Jr.; I must admit that black ants don't seem that pesky after all.

Stuffed Mushrooms Marcasi

1 lb large mushrooms- caps set aside; stems removed & chopped
4 slices white bread-torn into small pieces
1 small clove garlic-minced
½ tsp. oregano
½ cup Romano cheese
1 egg
2-Tbsp. oil

Mix bread, chopped mushrooms, garlic, egg, cheese, salt & pepper and oil.

Brush a shallow pan with oil. Stuff the caps piling high.

Bake at 350° for about 30 minutes or until brown and crunchy on top.

Raising Greed May 22, 2014

The other day my little guy returned from school carrying a fund-raiser form for kids with serious ailments and begged me to donate "just a hundred dollars". It was for a good cause; I felt happy that my kindergartner too felt invested in this noble mission until I heard him say that a hundred dollars would get him "the Super Cool Penguin". Upon further questioning, he enthusiastically rattled off all the enticing prizes that a different amount of donation would earn him: the Ninja Duck, the Gym Duck, the Pirate Duck and of course- the ultimate Snowboarding Penguin! Needless to say, the pride that I had felt was hopelessly squashed and after delivering a serious lesson in morals, I began to think about this much too common and unfair sales pitch.

I get it-- schools and organizations try to boost contributions by "bribing" kids with tangible items but I have a serious problem with that. Here is one of the best teachable moments to instill in our children unadulterated values of compassion and selflessness yet we choose to turn this into a selfish, self-serving and apathetic give and take. Why can't kids be told that they should donate simply because others are not as fortunate as they are, whether financially or physically, and because this is the only right thing to do? No glory, no expectation, only much-needed altruism.

The next week, I did send in a check-- not so much for the critter as for the cause. Within days the paltry penguin was lost along with a precious prospect at character building. I tried to do my part but it takes a village...

Pan Fried Ravioli

1 cup of flour
1 cup of breadcrumbs

3 eggs
½ cup of milk
A bag of frozen cheese ravioli, thawed
1 cup of vegetable oil
Marinara sauce

Beat the eggs with milk.
Dip the raviolis in the following order:
Flour
Egg/milk mixture
Bread crumbs.

Heat oil in pan. Fry on each side until golden brown. Serve with marinara sauce.

Red, White & GREEN May 29, 2014

Another Memorial Day has passed, leaving behind it a beautiful promise of warm, sunny days. How ironic that this day is meant to be a remembrance of those who will never see the sun rise again. An honorable tribute to our unparalleled heroes, yet do you know how millions of Americans "honored" those who hunted down our enemies and fought to their last drop? We hunted down bargains and shopped till we dropped. A dishonorable tribute indeed…

Melissa Johnson, a co-worker & friend, shared the following guilt-free, delicious recipe from "Clean Eating" Magazine. A heart-felt **Thank You** also to Mrs. Johnson's brother, Sergeant Brian McCormick, for honorably serving in the United States Army for the past nine years. We salute you and value your commitment!

Spaghetti Squash and Chicken

(Serves 4)
Ingredients
3 lb. spaghetti squash (quartered and seeded)
1 Bosc Pear, sliced
1 Tsp. dried sage
1lb chicken, cut into bite size pieces
3 oz. Parmesan cheese
1Tsp. oil

Preheat oven to 375°. Put quartered spaghetti squash into foiled 9x13 baking dish with about 1" of water. Put in oven for ½ hour or until a knife slides in easily.

Take out the squash and let it rest. Heat a deep sauté pan with oil and add the chicken. Sauté for about 2-3 minutes, flip the chicken; add the sage and pear. Sauté for about 5 minutes or until chicken has started to brown (and cooked through). While chicken is cooking, shred the squash with a fork and add to chicken mixture. Toss with chicken to deglaze the pan. Remove from heat and add the Parmesan cheese. Toss everything until cheese has coated the mixture. Garnish with a little extra cheese and enjoy!

Tough Cookie June 6, 2014

It felt like I was being stalked. It was the most disconcerting feeling even though those following me were 1) a women's garment, which shall remain unnamed out of deference for our male readers, and 2) a bicycle rack.

Here's what happened: A few days ago, I was watching an infomercial (I confess that these utterly inane "paid, commercial programs" can sometimes have the most mesmerizing effect). When it ended, I made a loyal trip to their website and the mistake of putting a few of the unnamed products in my shopping cart. I never made it to checkout; I was content that my cart was brimming with pretty things. End of story or so I thought.

A few days later I did an online search for a bike rack for my VW. Again, I the optimistic bargain hunter did a comparison shopping, adding 3 different kinds of racks into my shopping cart- to be decided later. And once again, "later" never came and I forgot about it until recently when the evil rack managed to attach itself to me thereby following me wherever I went.

When this first happened- I must admit I was very nervous. It started out with the garments; I was innocently talking to a friend online when the garments appeared and suggested that I get them. And then they were everywhere, joined intermittently by the rack. Once a hitch turned up and suggested that it would pair perfectly with "my rack". When I nervously asked my husband, who always has the answers when my computer is misbehaving (though I was certain that this time he would direct me to an Exorcist), he explained to me that it was only a "cookie" that stores a shopper's information as chips, follows a consumer around and is quite harmless.

I felt dated and remembered good times when the only kind of chip that a cookie stored was made of chocolate, *I* was the one who followed it around and even though it was not completely harmless, it was quite delicious to consume. I miss the olden days when cookies were stored in a cookie jar and not in a browser...

Old-fashioned Boy Scouts Oatmeal Cookies

¾ cup vegetable shortening
1 cup firmly packed brown sugar
½ cup granulated sugar
1 egg
¼ cup water
1 tsp. vanilla
3 cups uncooked oatmeal
1 cup all-purpose flour
1 tsp. salt
½ tsp. baking soda

Preheat oven to 350°. Cream together: shortening, sugars, egg, vanilla and water together until creamy. Add the flour, salt, and baking soda and finally, the oats. Drop the batter by teaspoonful onto greased cookie sheets and bake for 12-15 minutes.

Parched June 13, 2014

The vending machine had just ingested my quarters; I was hot, thirsty and coinless. I made my way to the Food Court next to the machine to see if I could retrieve my coins or at least get a bottle of water. Ordinarily I wouldn't have bothered but after a long day of running around, I desperately needed a drink. The line was long and as I made eye contact with the nice server gesturing that all I needed was a quick answer, she politely beckoned me to come. Almost instantaneously, a well-dressed, big man stepped forward, and pointing at me with his long fingers (and pointy beard) asked in the most unpleasant tone, "*What are you doing*?" I was taken aback at the rudeness in his voice and sheepishly said, "I am just asking a question." Still snickering, he stared at me piercingly and somewhat threatened by his arrogance I retreated to the back of the line. It was not worth fighting and quite frankly-- I was a bit scared.

Soon the cold water quenched my thirst but the heated interaction left a sour taste in my mouth. How impatient have we become that we cannot let someone ahead of us even for a minute. How utterly rude and uncaring have we become that we don't think twice about talking down to another. Forget chivalry- whatever happened to basic decency -- I sadly wondered. I felt small but recovered soon thereafter as I remembered the priceless words of Khalil Gibran-- "To belittle, you have to be little." The big guy was not so big after all...

A Last Minute Dinner Idea

I came up with this recipe when one evening I found only the following in my fridge:

1 bunch of asparagus

Portabella Mushrooms

Scallions

1 onion

and a package of fully-cooked chicken sausage (the kind that comes in a number of varieties). I took a blind leap of faith combining everything (& grabbing a few staples from the pantry) and believe it or not, this recipe has become a favorite in my house!

In a large skillet, heat about 1 Tbsp. of oil.

Add a pinch of red pepper flakes (optional) and a roughly chopped onion. Add the cut asparagus and Portabella mushrooms and let cook over high heat. Add the sausage pieces (diagonally cut) and mix well. Turn the heat down to medium and add a pinch of Chinese 5 spice powder, a Tbsp. of oyster sauce and a Tsp. of soy sauce. Season with salt & pepper. Sprinkle with roughly chopped pieces of scallions. Serve with rice. Surprisingly good!

Super Teacher June 19, 2014

One of the most enduring gifts of the Vedic era of ancient India was the Gurukul system (Guru- teacher, Kul- extended family), where the pupils lived in close proximity to their teacher until the age of 25 and received a holistic education. Along with imparting knowledge, it was the Guru's sacred duty to build character. Although Gurukul is a relic of the past, its vestiges remain, and teachers are held in high regard even to this day in modern India.

The West looks at educators through a different lens; teachers here are regarded more as service providers than objects of reverence. Having lived in both places, I can unequivocally say that even though the West and the East view and treat its educators differently, the educator is exactly the same in both worlds. This is one profession, which comes, as close as possible, to being spiritual. There is no ulterior motive; the educator does not seek a slice of success or a claim to fame that her pupils achieve, even though he is primarily responsible for both. A teacher's biggest reward is that the young soul, however disturbed or gifted, grows up to become a productive member of society and passes it on to the next generation some day.

So in this new world of ambitious ideas- the "race to the top" and its accouterments, undoubtedly putting a lot of undue pressure on the educator, let's "race to the basics" and not lose sight of the most important player in all of this- the ordinary teacher with an extraordinary responsibility and an accompanying genuine desire to fulfill it.

As another school year draws to a close I am reminded of this timeless quote by Mustafa Kemal Ataturk: "A good teacher is like a candle - it consumes itself to light the way for others."

So here's to the countless good teachers -- the amazing Gurus-- around me who burn brightly and light up the lives of young, impressionable minds and shape their tomorrows. Thank you!

The above column is lovingly dedicated to Mrs. Theresa Hagerty, a gem of a teacher who is retiring from the Canton Public Schools after years of selfless service. You will be greatly missed Mrs. Hagerty!

Aunt Connie's Kielbasa Hor'deurves

2 Pounds Kielbasa cooked and sliced about ½" thick.

Mix 8 ounces apple jelly and 8 ounces of Guldens mustard in a saucepan. Heat until the jelly melts. Pour over Kielbasa and reheat.

"Let's Move!" June 26, 2014

President Obama's exercise routine, secretly recorded & leaked while attending the G7 Summit in Poland this month, became the object of intense scrutiny on our nation's airwaves. While I respect the freedom of expression, I would like to express to the Pundits who indulged in this downright daffy disclosure, that granting the right to privacy, to even the most important public personality, is sometimes only right.

May I also politely remind them that this undue attention on the President's gym moves and his bench presses instead of on pressing foreign and domestic moves is downright dismal? And that responsible and classy expression, otherwise known as judicious journalism, this *ain't*?

The following recipe comes from Marianne Arcieri, a wonderful mom, health expert and the founder of "Little Flowers". It is, hands-down, the best pizza I have ever tasted. Marianne writes:

"I started experimenting with gourmet pizzas when Michael and I first got married. The Eggplant Pizza is my favorite creation. It's been a hit with every one I make it for and I'm glad you enjoyed it. I hope you have many healthy and happy years drinking wine and eating eggplant pizza with friends and family!

Eggplant Pesto and Caramelized onion Pizza

1. Any pizza dough of your choice.
2. 2-3 tbsp. of pesto - spread over the dough.
3. Cut and bake two medium size eggplants, careful not to over cook the eggplant.
4. Cut one large Vidalia onion, sauté

5. Sprinkle 1- cup of mozzarella cheese over the caramelized onions.

To assemble the pizza:

Roll out your dough onto a pizza board, cover with flour or corn flour so your dough slides off the board. Make sure the size of dough you are working with is manageable for you; it can be tricky placing the heavy pizza in the oven on your stone. Next spread the pesto over the dough, not too much or it will run in your oven. After the eggplant has cooled, layer it over the dough, you can overlap the eggplant a little if you like. Next place only the caramelized onions over the eggplant. Lastly, your choice of cheese: Marianne's favorite (& mine): goat cheese and mozzarella together.

Give it a try!

Brakes Please July 4, 2014

Recently I was trailing my little guy as he was learning to ride his bike. The training wheels must have made him feel invincible for he decided to race down a hilly street in spite of mom's frantic pleas. "But I love hills and NO, I won't get hurt"- were the last words I heard before the thud of a crash. Panic-stricken, I rushed, barely managing to catch a flying child as his helmeted head hit the sidewalk! My heart raced a mile a minute as I gathered up my little mess to survey the hurt caused by his reckless rebellion. With a tiny scrape over his eye came a promise- "I will never do that again; I am sorry, I will always listen to you mom". My heart sank at the sight of the bruised child but at the same time I realized how lucky I was that it was a short-lived pain, for my baby and me. At that moment I could not help but think of so many moms just like me whose grown babies are headed down the hill a little too fast for comfort with no second chance.

Josh's Chicken Torta

A Mexican bolillo roll cut in half and lightly grilled face down.

Take roll and coat bottom with 4 oz pinto beans with bacon.

Add 4 oz of chicken.

Take 4 oz of cheese & fry. Place on top of carne asada.

Add pico de gallo, jalapeño sauce, shredded lettuce.

Take other half of roll and spread 2 oz of guacamole.

Then place sandwich together and place on flat top for 1 min on each side.

Cut in half and ready to serve.

You may try making the Torta at home or better still, take a trip to the Taqueria tonight!

Can't Take It No More   July 10, 2014

People get so aggravated for nothing. Today I got all worked up when the fast food joint mixed up my order. I was aggravated enough to yell at a total stranger, who, I admit now, was doing a fine job trying to cater to my whims and the whims of a million needy others like me. So what if I did get the ice that I didn't ask for, so what if I didn't get the extra ketchup that I asked for, so what if the chicken was not extra crispy, so what, so what, so what? I wish we would get just as aggravated because children are starving and because innocence is being abused while we are busy catering to our whims and fancy. I wish we could get aggravated enough to yell and make a difference.

Banana Ripple Cake

A great way to use up the bananas sweltering in the summer heat!

½ cup chocolate bits
¼ cup water
2 cups flour
¾ Tsp. baking soda
½ Tsp. salt
¼ Tsp. baking powder
½ cup butter
1-1/2 cups sugar
2 eggs separated
1 cup mashed bananas
⅓-cup sour cream
1 Tsp. vanilla
⅓ cup chopped maraschino cherries

Grease and flour the bottom of a 9" or 10" tube pan. Melt chocolate bits over water on low heat until smooth. Cool.

Combine flour, baking soda, salt and baking powder. Set aside.

In a separate bowl, cream the butter and gradually add the sugar. Beat until light and fluffy. Add egg yolks and beat well. Combine bananas, sour cream and vanilla. Add alternately to the creamed mixture with the dry ingredients and blend well. Stir in the cherries.

Beat egg whites until small mounds form. Gradually add ½ cup sugar and beat until stiff. Fold into batter.

Pour ⅓ of the batter into the pan. Follow with ½ of chocolate mixture. Repeat, ending with the batter.

Bake at 350° for 50-60 minutes. Cool in pan.

Glaze: Brown 2 Tbsps. of butter lightly. Blend in 1 cup of confectioner's sugar, ½ Tsp. vanilla and 2 to 3 Tbsp. milk. Drizzle over the cake.

Thanks Aunt Connie for your gift of sweetness!

A Modern Fairy Tale July 17, 2014

On Friday, I came home, once again, complaining about being so tired that I could barely move. It had been a long, hard week! My family, going to a Revs Screening Party, begged me to go with them, with the unselfish intent of spending Friday night together. I told them I just couldn't this time for I was exhausted beyond words. Watching me drag myself around the house and then collapse on the bed, they took pity and urged me no more.

As I watched the wheels get out of the driveway, the wheels in my head started to turn. I had three whole hours to myself and to spend them cooped up at home would be sacrilegious! The victorious feeling of freedom and the accompanying sight of pretty things that followed as soon as the car pulled out cured my exhaustion almost immediately. So I jumped up like a bolt of lightning, got dressed in a jiffy and drove off in my car at the speed of light --headed straight to the Shoppes.

As I walked around savoring every minute of my noisy solitude, I felt like Cinderella at the (mall) ball who like the fairy tale character had to be home before midnight, only this time instead of turning into a modest maiden I would have to transform into a distressed damsel. So right before the clock struck 10, I pulled into my driveway, changed into the shabbiest clothes and jumped into my bed with a fierce Olympian dive.

When the family came in they found poor Cinderella curled up in bed exhausted. I heard ruffled footsteps and hushed whispers reminding the boys not to disturb poor mom who lay there with the covers drawn (and the slippers hidden in the closet)! Mom sure was exhausted but for reasons that were best kept under wraps....

Jimmy's Easy Lentil Soup (serves 4)

Boil 1 Pound of lentils in water for 15 minutes, drain; fill with fresh water.

Put in white onion, finely chopped 4 cloves of garlic and black pepper. After boiling for 45 minutes, add fresh crushed tomatoes and boil for 15 minutes more, or bypass the tomatoes and add a few splashes of extra virgin olive oil. Jimmy Dimitrios of Pizza Market Fame in Sharon adds, "No need to add salt- the flavor comes from veggies". (Quite a shocker for someone who worships salt)!

Good Night, Sweet Dreams July 24, 2014

I think the reason why my kids (and yours) fight going to bed and ward off sleep is because they do not need to dream yet; they are certain that their dreams are meant to be some day— just like I did not so long ago. Today I love it when suddenly, in the middle of nothing spectacular at the end of a long day, I realize that I am dog-tired. I am the happiest when I can no longer keep my eyes open; I easily give in when the time comes for me to bid farewell to another ordinary day. That's when I rush to bed hoping to dream of extraordinary things that were meant to be some day.

Who says dreams don't come true?

Jay's Dreamy Coconut Soup

1-Tbsp. butter
2-cups whole milk
½ cup shredded coconut (unsweetened)
1-cup coconut milk
2 Tbsp. each of almonds and cashews

In a deep saucepan, heat butter. Sauté coconut on low flame and then add the nuts. Stir well. (Do not brown or burn). Add remaining ingredients and simmer until warm. Put everything in a blender and add a hint of nutmeg. Enjoy!

The Best Burger Bar (Your Own Backyard) July 31, 2014

Trust me when I say that you can make the best burgers at home; the secret is in the toppings. You can form your own patties with a little bit of salt and pepper or buy store-bought ones. I personally love Sam's Choice available at Wal-Mart. They come in a variety of flavors but my favorite happens to be the Black Angus Bacon and Smoked Cheddar Premium Patties. Spruce up your choice of burgers with my favorite toppings--preferably all of the following:

Romaine Lettuce

Thinly sliced red onions

Thinly sliced tomatoes

Jarred Banana Peppers (Take a handful, drain & dry them on a paper towel, chop and add according to taste)

Crisped Bacon strips

Avocados- sliced and drizzled with lime juice so they don't turn brown

Cheese slices

Whole-wheat buns-- Buttered & Toasted

Make a mixture of mayo, ketchup and Dijon mustard and apply sparsely on top bun.

Top burger with the toppings and enjoy with a generous heaping of the following:

Best Potato Salad

Ingredients
5 Pounds red potatoes, skin on- boiled until tender (Do not overcook)
Salt
About 5/6 strips of bacon (cooked and chopped and ¼ cup grease reserved)
1 cup finely chopped bell pepper (I like yellow and red))
1 small minced red onion
1 bunch of thinly sliced scallions
¼ cup olive oil
4 Tbsp. red wine vinegar
3 -Tbsp. Dijon Mustard
3 Tbsp. Mayonnaise
Salt & pepper

Directions

In a large bowl, combine the potatoes, bacon, bell pepper, onion and scallions.

In a bowl, whisk the olive oil, bacon bits scraped along with the bacon grease, vinegar, mustard, mayonnaise, 1-Tbsp. salt and 1 Tsp. pepper. Mix in with the potatoes. Cover and refrigerate or serve at room temperature. (Always taste for seasonings especially salt).

Bitter Reality August 1, 2014

As I am seated on a plane headed 8000 miles away, the most surreal thoughts crowd my mind and I ask her:

How *does one* come to terms with the bitter truth that:

The strongest woman in the world has no more strength left?

The one you depended on for every decision all your life can no longer decide and will depend on you for what is left of hers?

The little things that you took for granted through childhood and adulthood are a thing of the past, *never* to be attained again?

How *do you* grow up when the heart says you are still her little girl?

How *can* you come to grips with your most beloved and only selfless relationship slowly withering away?

All I hope and pray is that *IF* there is the God that she has so faithfully loved and worshipped through the best of times and the worst of suffering-- He is compassionate enough to spare her suffering in the time she has left.

Salmon and Spinach Fishcakes

1 cup frozen spinach, defrosted
16 butter crackers
About 2 cups or 16 oz. can Salmon chunks in brine, drained zest of 1 lemon
1 large egg, separated
2 Tbsp. freshly chopped parsley

4 Tbsp. olive oil
3 Tbsp. mayonnaise
2 Tbsp. whole grain mustard

Squeeze any excess water from the spinach and set aside.

Place 6 crackers in a food processor and blitz to make fine crumbs, then tip onto a flat plat and set aside for coating the fishcakes later.

Put the remaining crackers in a food processor and blitz until fine. Add in the Salmon, spinach, lemon zest, egg yolk, parsley and season with salt & pepper. Combine fully.

Put the egg white in a bowl and whisk.

Shape the salmon mixture into 6 patties, dip each one into the egg white, then coat in the reserved cracker crumbs.

Heat the oil in a frying pan over medium heat and cook the fish cakes for 5 minutes on each side, until perfectly golden. Meanwhile mix the Mayonnaise and mustard in a small bowl. Serve the fish cakes hot with the dip. (Adapted from Arabia Food & Travel Magazine).

Neil August 8, 2014

Today I witnessed something that I wish upon not even my worst enemy. I saw crippling pain that most of us will never (& I hope will never) experience. I saw a mother grieving for her only child who was ripped from her bosom. I saw a father trying to hold his unbearable pain inside of him so he could appear strong for his loving wife (but in the course of that day, I saw him physically shudder several times- which a family member explained to me afterwards, happens involuntarily while he silently remembers and grieves for his beloved son).

This is what happened-- as I was getting ready to return to India to take care of my ailing mother, a tragedy of epic proportions unfolded in our family. My twenty-four year old cousin suddenly died from a ruptured ulcer.

I am aware that death is a fact of life, but when death comes knocking unexpectedly to take away the nicest young man from the two most amazing human beings, it is a bitter fact that is hard to swallow. Neil was an ideal young man; he was- hands down- the nicest person I have known- smart, jolly, responsible, kind and wise beyond words with an uncanny fondness of stray animals and the elderly. His sense of duty and his maturity were well beyond his tender years and it was his unshakable faith in God that drove him to do extraordinary acts of kindness. (I often joked and teased him for being such an old soul and a saint). I could go on and on about the things he did but will, for now, keep them buried deep inside and probably draw from his examples to do some small good in this world when I am ready). I will confess though that my faith has been shattered since this tragedy; a sweet friend of mine kindly explained to me that God needs the best human beings by His side, which is why He took Neil away. With all due respect, I believe this is bologna;

God is supposed to be kind, not mercilessly cruel and selfish. If you have a better answer, would you please share with me so I can regain some sanity and a bit of faith? I know this is not about me but I desperately need something to hold on to and pass on to his parents who are left with nothing but a life full of unforgettable memories and unforgiving pain. Perhaps someone has an answer….

Mint Tea Cocktail

4 Peppermint tea bags
1 handful mint leaves
2 Tbsp. sugar
1 cup of ice cubes
1 lime, sliced
1 lemon sliced
Gin

In a large saucepan, bring a litre or about 4¾ cups of water to a boil. Remove from heat and add tea bags and mint leaves. Allow to steep for approximately 5 minutes before removing them. Add sugar and let dissolve. Allow to cool before decanting into a jug. Put in refrigerator to chill.

Once thoroughly chilled add ice along with the gin. To serve pour the chilled cocktail into glasses and garnish with lemon and lime slices and mint leaves.

Enjoy the occasional sweet things in life friends for life is too short.

Human August 15, 2014

I put Ten Rupees, the equivalent of 20 cents, in the shriveled hand of a frail, old lady on the street. She touched my feet- the ultimate sign of respect- clearly overwhelmed by this simple gesture and visibly happy that at least *a* meal was guaranteed for *that* day. Such an appreciation for what should be the birth right of every human being! "What justice!" - I lamented as I carelessly tossed my half-eaten sandwich in the trash and walked away to my life of comfort.

Chicken Saltimbocca with Ham & Marsala

4 medium skinless, boneless chicken breasts
4 slices of raw aged ham cut in half widthways
8 large sage leaves
6-Tbsp. olive oil
¼ stick butter
¾ cup Marsala

Put the chicken breasts on a chopping board between two sheets of cling wrap. Use a mallet to flatten them into escalopes about 1 cm thick.

Cut the escalopes in half widthwise to get 8 pieces in total. Season with salt & pepper and lay a piece of ham on each piece. Top with one sage leaf and secure with a toothpick.

Heat the oil and half the butter in a large frying pan over medium heat. Place the saltimbocca in the pan, ham side down. Cook for 2 minutes until browned. Turn and cook for additional 3 minutes until just cooked through. Transfer to a platter and cover with foil.

Pour the Marsala into the hot pan carefully; let cook and deglaze the pan by scraping the meaty bits from the bottom.

Simmer over high heat for a minute until slightly reduced. Stir in the remaining butter and check for seasoning.

Return the chicken and any juices to the pan, turning them in the sauce for 30 seconds. Remove the pan from the heat and the toothpicks from the chicken.

Place two pieces of saltimbocca on each serving plate and drizzle with the Marsala sauce. Enjoy!

Recipe modified from "Arabia Food and Travel magazine".

The More You Have… August 22, 2014

I gave my teenage son 6 pairs of brand new socks in September; by December most of them had managed to make a getaway from his closet. Of course, he blamed the socks for losing him. On returning to India just days ago, I was touched to see our domestic help's son proudly sporting my son's old pair, which I had given him 2 years ago. His mom informed me that the young boy took great pride in & even greater care of his socks, taking them out on special occasions only. Grateful at this simple act of receiving this seemingly insignificant hand-me-down, she was convinced that he would have those "special" socks forever.

At that otherwise insignificant moment I realized that the less you have the more you have….

Lamb cutlets coated with Pancetta and Parmesan

(Chicken or Veal cutlets would work too)

- 2 ounces pancetta, finely chopped
- 1-cup breadcrumbs
- 3 Tbs. freshly grated Parmesan
- 12 lamb cutlets, preferably French-trimmed (ask the butcher to do this)
- 2 large eggs, beaten
- 6-Tbsp. olive oil

Mix together the ham, Parmesan cheese and breadcrumbs in a large bowl; set aside.

Dip each cutlet first into the beaten eggs and then coat with breadcrumb mixture. Press the cutlets firmly into the mixture so it coats the surface evenly.

Heat the oil in large frying pan over medium heat. Cook cutlets in hot oil for 3 minutes on each side. Transfer them onto paper towels to absorb excess oil. Season with salt & pepper. Serve with a simple salad and warm bread.

This recipe is modified from "Arabia- Food and Travel".

Happy Travels September 4, 2014

I am an experienced traveler. I like to think of myself as a classy one too but something happens every time I am on a plane-I go from being dumb to dumber.

Recently, I found myself sitting next to a young man- a businessman type from Johannesburg. Being a polished and experienced traveler, he quickly made himself comfortable while I, started fumbling around for my missing headphones, which I had held just minutes ago. The fun began after eventually locating them tucked away in a corner of my seat (how?) for now I could not find the outlet to plug them in. I surreptitiously tried every hole within sight so that my neighbor would not catch my antics (& misses). I finally succeeded to plug them in but this time, could not work the remote. (By this time my fellow traveler was well into his second movie). I decided to try later- -I was convinced that after his many drinks he would soon pass out leaving me free to try even harder; moreover it was dinnertime. Trying to appear cool (although *no one* cared), I opted for the vegetarian menu from a choice of two amazing meaty entrees, which I began to regret right away. The stewardess' smirk should have warned me-- the lone rice pilaf came garnished with charred onions and burned cashews. Just my luck but at least this time it was not my fault!

Next I reached for the inviting mini focaccia to go with the Mediterranean Dip but could not open the plastic wrapper. After an hour-long struggle with the packet, I had failed to rip it but successfully managed to make focaccia crumbs. The story repeated itself with the butter crackers that accompanied the sweet chili relish; this time I got cracker crumbs plus blisters.

Why is it that I was acting more drunk without consuming a single drop of alcohol while my co-passenger remained collected while drinking Heineken after Heineken and downing pretty little bottles of spirits?

My spirit lifted as I caught a glimpse of the irresistible, bite-size candy bar in its shiny blue wrapper. Finally- exactly what I needed after all the madness I had experienced! I closed my eyes and popped the creamy goodness into my mouth. The next minute the cool, composed, classy me was crudely spitting out the "Land O Lakes Salted Butter". "Planely" I had outdone myself yet again...

Baba Ghanoush (Recipe modified from Inflight Magazine)

4 eggplants (or aubergines as they are called in Arabia)
2 garlic cloves, crushed
1 lemon juice, squeezed
1 tbsp. tahini
3 tbsp. olive oil

Preheat oven to 400°. Put the eggplants on a greased baking sheet, side by side and roast in the preheated oven for about 30 minutes or until the skins are blistered and charred. Remove from the oven and leave to cool.

Once cool, scrape off their flesh into a mixing bowl, discarding the charred skins. Add the garlic, lemon juice, tahini and oil. Using a fork, mash up the flesh until everything is well incorporated into a chunky puree. Season with salt & pepper. Garnish with cilantro. Enjoy with flatbread or mini focaccia!

Thank You! September 11, 2014

Today I wanted to take some time to thank all of you who have written to me about my recent columns. I cannot begin to tell you how much hearing from good friends, acquaintances and complete strangers has helped me get through some very difficult times and sort through previously unknown feelings. I must admit that I was uncertain about publishing the very personal articles, especially the one about Neil. I had written it as a way of dealing with my own grief and Jay, our wonderful editor, once again had the foresight to suggest that I share it. I am glad he did…

When an unthinkable tragedy occurs, we often get blindsided and sometimes lose the ability to reason. I being a somewhat private person have never been certain as to how to deal with pain publicly and in the past have felt that it is worthless to discuss it especially with someone who was not part of it to start with. I have learnt, thanks to you, that just like joy doubles when you share it with others, pain too lessens greatly when you let others in on it.

There is so much I have learnt in the past weeks about the resilience of the human spirit. I have learnt for the first time how some of you that I have loved and respected for years and who never stop smiling, have endured horrific losses in your personal lives. I have learnt how many of you have risen above personal tragedies and instead of burying the grief, have used it to bring meaning and joy to others. I have learnt that in spite of life being very tough at times, it is the kindness of those around us that makes it livable. I have cherished reading about your personal experiences, about your advice and suggestions.

Pastor Baril's beautiful letter gives me chills every time I read it; Ann's invaluable resource- "When Bad Things

Happen To Good People" by Harold S. Kushner has become a Godsend. I was deeply touched to hear from Robin, who is my good friend Bernard Mendillo's beautiful wife and with whom I have never corresponded before. I truly appreciated her genuine concern and something else, which I will share with you. Her simple email made me smile

Robin, after sharing some genuine thoughts, writes:

"...On a brighter note, Bernie mentioned you were interested in recipes -- and I've got lots of them!

Here's one. This is adapted from Marcella Hazan's famous cookbook 'The Essentials of Classic Italian Cooking'.

It's so easy and so dependable. They will never have to buy jar sauce again!

Tomato with Onion & Butter Sauce:

1 can of tomatoes (I prefer the plum and not the "Kitchen Ready").

1 sweet white onion cut in half.

5 Tbsp. unsalted butter

1 Tsp. salt

1-1½ Lbs. pasta

(Serves 4 - 6 people)

Grind tomatoes in processor or blender.

Place in saucepan.

Add peeled white onion, butter and salt.

Cook on slow low heat for at least 45 minutes. Taste and correct for salt.

After draining the pasta, add a couple of tablespoons of butter to pasta -- and serve with sauce.

Serve with grated cheese.

Note: You can remove onion and save for another time or eat it. And most important -- kids will NOT taste the onion. Trust me on this one! :)

And that's it! I serve this alone with a salad or sometimes with sausages on the grill.

Easy and delicious -- especially for quick back to school dinners!

Take care, Rumni~

Robin"

Yes- recipes make me happy and so does hearing from you- so keep them coming!

With love and gratitude,

Rumni

In Memory of September 19, 2014

The savage assassinations of James Foley and Steven Sotloff are brutal reminders of what misguided feelings of nationalism and religious zeal can lead to. A vicious crime is often the result of impaired judgment brought about by external factors but sometimes, as in this case, the culprit is a far worse offender. There is no substance or illness more powerful than what some harbor in their hearts-pure and unadulterated feelings of hatred stemming from irreconcilable differences and often, the most inane premise that "My God is better than yours".

Religion is what sets us humans apart from other animals; religion is supposed to sober us and bring us together; yet some of the most heinous crimes are committed in the name of religion and often, "my God" is what separates me from you.

How does one have so much hatred that he does not wince while casually slitting the throat of another human being? How is one so blinded by his beliefs that he can justify callously and brutally beheading a living, breathing fellow being? What has humanity disintegrated into? If this is Evolution of man, I shudder to think where mankind is headed. In its deepest level, these inhumane killings are about our utter failure as human beings to empathize with and feel for others. Unfortunately, in this era of progress and modernity, some of us are humans no more.

The above article is dedicated to innocence lost on September 11, 2001.

Ratatouille

4-Tbsp. olive oil
2 onions, diced
2 garlic cloves, crushed
2 eggplants, diced
3 zucchini, diced
2 red peppers, diced
16 oz. can of whole, peeled, tomatoes

A handful of fresh basil, roughly chopped

Heat the oil in a large pan and sauté the onions until softened; add the garlic over low heat for a few minutes.

Add the eggplants, zucchini and peppers.

Add the tomatoes and basil. Stir thoroughly, then cover pan with lid and simmer gently for 10-15 minutes.

Add salt & pepper to taste and serve with crusty bread to mop up the juices.

Tip: Save or freeze leftovers to add over spaghetti with freshly grated Parmesan and a drizzle of olive oil.

Recipe adapted from “Friday” Magazine.

Much Too Soon Sept 25, 2014

I realize that the most precious commodity in life is also the one that is absolutely free but because there is so much of it all at once- we do not give it the time of day. The most valuable thing I realize more and more is good old time.

We do not give time due respect till we run out of it and run out of it- we all do, no matter who we are or how much power we wield.

Time does not discriminate; time is blind. We often talk about "managing time", which is really our vanity talking, for it is the other way around. Time manages us. We all are in a race against time knowing fully well that we can never win. For years we squander away time because there is so much of it and then one day, out of the blue, it hits us that everything in life has a life span- even time.

Here's a simple example from my own life- all these years I took my time with my mom for granted. All I saw was never-ending time with her and therefore did not give her the time that she deserved; she was always there and would be there for me whenever I needed her--- or so I erroneously thought. Today, all of a sudden, mom is fast running out of time.

Today I wish I could say that I have nothing but time. Today I am suddenly reminded of Dr. Seuss' timeless words: *"How did it get so late so soon?"*

Tarragon Chicken

1 Tbsp. each of butter and olive oil
2 chicken breasts
1 shallot, thinly sliced
1 garlic clove, crushed

4 Tbsp. chopped tarragon, plus extra for garnishing
3 Tbsp. crème fraiche

Sautéed potatoes, to serve

Heat the butter and oil in a pan and sauté the chicken breasts on both sides until lightly golden. Cover the pan, reduce the heat and cook for 8-10 minutes.

Push the chicken to the side, add the shallots and garlic and cook for 1-2 minutes. Add the tarragon and crème fraiche and cook for 1 minute.

Season with salt and pepper and serve with potato wedges sautéed in olive oil. Simple and delicious!

*Save the crème fraiche for a dessert recipe in next week's paper.

Recipe adapted from "Friday" Magazine

Love it or Leave it October 2, 2014

A good friend of mine recently broke up with her long-time love. Seemed like the couple had everything going for them; yet something was obviously missing. People talk; I have heard hushed whispers about how someone could throw away a good thing. To that I say- we only live once and if my lovely lady friend had the gumption to demand more out of life, more power to her!

I think we often judge others because we don't have the audacity to do what they do or the guts to change our lives; we often settle for less than what we desire because that's the only easy thing to do.

As long as one is not deliberately hurting another, I see no wrong in wanting more out of life. Life is over in the blink of an eye, life is what dictates its terms to us- so be demanding when you can and make life work for you. Don't let anyone tell you what to do, don't ever be satisfied with less than satisfactory. Listen to your heart and remember- whatever you do, be happy, my friend.

Love,
Rumni

Tarte Fine Aux Pommes (It's French for Apple Tart)

3 Granny Smith apples
Juice of 1 lemon
14/16 oz. ready made puff pastry, defrosted
5-Tbsp. melted butter
2-Tbsp. brown sugar

Peel, core and thinly slice the apples. Toss the apple slices with the lemon juice to ensure they do not get brown.

Preheat the oven to 350°. Grease a baking tray.

Roll out the pastry and use a cookie cutter to cut it into 6 circles.

Place each circle on the tray, making sure that they don't touch each other.

Arrange the apple slices on top of the pastry in a flower pattern, overlapping.

Drizzle the butter over the apples. Mix together cinnamon and sugar and sprinkle it evenly over the apples.

Bake for 12 minutes or until golden brown. Do not open the oven door while the tarts are baking.

Cool slightly. Dust with powdered sugar and serve with crème fraiche.

Easier done than said!

Recipe adapted from "Friday" Magazine.

Enough Already! October 9, 2014

While it is not clear whether the rogue Islamic organization wants to be called ISIS, ISIL or just IS, there is no denying the fact that it is made up of ruthless killers who will go to barbaric lengths to promote their frenzied cause.

Recently we all waited with bated breath for President Obama to announce a strategy to deal with this growing menace. The President came up with a practical and more conservative tactic of targeted allied attacks combined with the training of local forces to combat this unforgiving, extremist group. After all, it is not the responsibility of America alone to hunt down these insurgents; others around the world have just as much of a vested interest and an inescapable duty to do their part in weeding out these miscreants. A full out war against a reclusive group such as this is just not feasible. And how easily we forget the unnecessary legacy of the Iraq war. Saddam is long gone but revolting hatred toward America stemming from the war has been ingrained for generations to come and given rise to thousands of radicals, including the ones making headlines today. (I was horrified to hear that it is Saddam's military that makes up a formidable part of ISIS today. Whatever happened to "Mission Accomplished"?)

Soon after the announcements, the airwaves and social networking sites lit up with callous criticism aimed at the Commander-in-Chief's strategy. And although I listened carefully to many an opinion, I must say that not one critiquing individual- professional or amateur- had a veritable solution or a viable suggestion in place of what the President outlined. It struck me then how easy it is to complain, criticize and whine and how it is even easier to dissect someone else's plan without contributing to it. Chuck Jones' simple, timeless piece of advice springs to life, like many of his Looney Tune cartoons: *"Anyone can negatively criticize - it is the cheapest of all comment because it requires not a modicum of the effort that suggestion requires"*. In the midst of our acrimony let's not lose sight of the bigger picture here-- America is under attack, let's not attack each other, folks!

Easy Side

In a hot pan add 1 Tbsp. each of butter and olive oil. Add 8 oz. mushroom, a bunch of trimmed asparagus and 2 cloves chopped garlic. Sauté for 5-6 minutes. Add a Tsp. of chopped parsley. Toss and put 1 tbsp. of Worcestershire sauce. Serve with meat or fish.

Scandalous October 16, 2014

The Ray Rice incident has the press agog with excitement and buzzing with opinions. While I, like most, do not have enough information to know what transpired that shameful evening, I will say this- anyone who has seen the surveillance video cannot be hoodwinked into believing that this was an unfortunate accident.

No matter what or who perpetrated the events, a man who loses self-control to the point that he punches his so-called love unconscious, and is then brazen enough to kick and drag her lifeless body, is no hero. I would perhaps, have been a little more patient and understanding had Mr. Rice appeared worrisome that he may have had inadvertently hurt his fiancée or caused her harm while she lay on the floor- unresponsive. How could one not be shocked at the sight of her limp head precariously nestled in between the elevator doors? His gut instinct should have been to get her out of harm's way but he appeared completely unfazed by it. It is not hard to see that this was perhaps not the first time that things had gotten out of hand; (un)fortunately this time there were prying eyes.

Ray Rice may be a wealthy guy with superior athletic prowess on the football field but his actions that day on the elevator floor blatantly showed that he is nothing but a poor man and an unfit, inferior coward. How easily can one spiral down from hero to zero in the all-important game of life!

Delicious Apple Cake

1& 3/4 cups sugar
3/4 - 1 cup vegetable oil
3 eggs
1 tsp. vanilla extract
1 tsp. salt
2 cups flour
1 tsp. baking soda
5 - 6 apples peeled, cored, and sliced

Preheat oven to 350 degrees F. Grease and flour 9 x 13 pan.

Whisk sugar into vegetable oil in a mixing bowl. Beat eggs, vanilla extract, salt, flour and baking soda into the sugar mixture 1 ingredient at a time. Fold apple slices into the batter: pour into the prepared baking dish.

Bake in the preheated oven until a toothpick inserted into the center comes out clean - 40 - 50 minutes.

Thanks to Diane Keverian for sharing the above recipe!

Alo(ha!) October 22, 2014

Recently, the Police Department in the Paradise Island created some epic waves. Ludicrous but true- for decades Hawaii has allowed undercover officers to legallyengage in intimate relationships with prostitutes in the course of their investigations. Quite an on-the-job perk, won't you agree? Recent legislation to ban this law, which the island experts claim is "necessary" to make their case against sex workers and human traffickers, was struck down thanks to massive lobbying efforts on the part of the officers. Seriously- how ***does*** one lobby for a Dionysian deal such as this?

Look- I have nothing but the utmost respect for our law enforcement but a provision such as this, no matter how much we try to justify it, benefits one party AND one party only. Moreover, how is it that the remaining 49 states are able to conduct business in a professional manner without turning into the John that they are after?

Appalling that a law as incredulous as this is actually alive in a civilized nation like ours! Any way you look at it- it is sexist, invasive and offensive.

The Paradise Island has been blessed with unsurpassed natural beauty- let's not tarnish it by preserving this unnatural ugliness.

Paradise Salad

1 bag of mixed salad greens
1-cup pomegranate
½-cup walnut pieces, toasted

1-cup of crisp apple chunks (cored & peeled)
¼ cup thinly slivered almonds

Toss everything together just before serving. (I like to add generous shavings of Parmesan).

Add a store-bought, good quality Vinaigrette. Enjoy!

Oh Me Oh My! October 30, 2014

The other day a good friend of mine told me that I never notice the most blatant of things. That same day, another friend commented that not even the littlest thing gets past me and that I don't ever miss a thing. Bizarre coincidence-- I wondered? The more I thought about it the more I realized that both of them, though holding diametrically opposing views, are one hundred percent correct for while I am completely oblivious to the obvious, I never fail to pick up the most obscure. I am not talking about important stuff mind you- just unnecessary, unimportant facts and marginally slanted human behaviors, mannerisms and eccentricities. I cannot read explicit directions or follow categorical instructions and most always fail to pay attention to what others are desperately trying to draw my attention to, yet if someone does something remotely odd, I remember it for the rest of my life. For instance, I remember vividly how my first grade music teacher's sneeze resembled the high pitch whistle of a flute. To this day I am debating whether it was her lyrical sneeze that prompted her to become a musician or she somehow trained her sneeze to be melodic. (No wonder I can't focus on the more hefty problems of life!)

Believe me when I say that this is a genuine problem, one that I have been afflicted with all my life. My mind is filled with random, useless information that I pick up along the way and which in turn makes me think random, useless thoughts. You may say that this is superficial but I say that someday when my life flashes before my eyes- I will still be laughing!

Cinderella Cake (Pumpkin- get it?)

Pinned & modified by my friend Sherrill D'Attanasio Morrison

2 cups sugar
4 eggs
1-cup vegetable oil
2 cups flour
2-Tsp. baking soda
2 Tsp. cinnamon
½ Tsp. salt
1-15 oz. can pumpkin puree
1 Tsp. vanilla
1-cup mini chocolate chips

Beat sugar and eggs till well blended. Add oil, continuing to beat. Combine dry ingredients to egg mixture. Add pumpkin and mix well. Add a cup of mini chocolate chips.

Bake at 350• for an hour. Super easy and super moist.

You may decorate with orange/black frosting and "glue" candy corns for a festive look!

Happy Halloween friends!

Let's never lose the childish innocence and the joy of the holidays!

Love,
Rumni

About the Author

Rumni Saha is an acclaimed newspaper columnist, a much-loved special needs teacher, and a dedicated family gal in a quiet suburb of Boston. She holds a masters degree in education from Boston University. Rumni writes and cooks with unfettered passion. Her stories are heartfelt, sensible, and often controversial yet always thought provoking. Her cooking style is simple, eclectic, and flavorful. "Cooking," she claims, "is not much different from teaching. Add some key ingredients, follow a few simple steps and always cook with love. The result is a recipe for success."